How to Get Lucky: How to Change Your Mind and Get Anything in Life

Dan Desmarques

Published by 22 Lions Publishing, 2021.

Table of Contents

Copyright Page 1

About 3

Introduction 5

Chapter 1 — The Opportunities You Ignore. 7

Chapter 2 — The Difference Between Dreamers and Fools. 11

Chapter 3 — How a Belief in Help Shapes Your Attitude. 13

Chapter 4 — The Greatest Fear in Us. 15

Chapter 5 — Change as a Natural Necessity. 17

Chapter 6 — How the Rich and the Poor Think. 21

Chapter 7 — Why I Travel So Much. 25

Chapter 8 — Using Your Dreams to Motivate You. 27

Chapter 9 — What is Money for You? 29

Chapter 10 — How to Change the Synapses in Your Brain. 31

Chapter 11 — How to Find The People You Need in Life 33

Chapter 12 — People Have a Short Memory. 37

Chapter 13 — The Influence of Time and Space. 39

Chapter 14 — How Karma Attracts the Right People. 41

Chapter 15 — Bad Experiences Can Lead to Positive Results. ... 43

Chapter 16 — You Won't Find God in a Religious Group. 45

Chapter 17 — God's Kingdom is Within You. 47

Chapter 18 — With God Everything is Possible. 49

Chapter 19 — How to Communicate With God....................................51

Chapter 20 — The Greatest Secret About Luck....................................55

Chapter 21 — Everyone Attracts Luck..59

Chapter 22 — You Can Change What Others Think of You............63

Chapter 23 — How to Control Your Mind..65

Chapter 24 — How to Control Your Emotions....................................69

Chapter 25 — Never Count on Support During Hard Times..........73

Chapter 26 — Why People Lose Their Luck and How to Get it Back............75

Chapter 27 — How to Change Your Personal Vibration....................77

Chapter 28 — Money Does Not Make People Evil.............................79

Chapter 29 — How to Uplift Your Emotions.......................................81

Chapter 30 — How to Master Success and Luck.................................83

Chapter 31 — Why Most Artists and Authors Have No Luck.........87

Chapter 32 — How to Avoid Failure..91

Chapter 33 — Luck as a Science..93

Chapter 34 — The Signs of Luck in the Environment.......................95

Chapter 35 — How Expectations Can Determine Results................97

Chapter 36 — Can We Relearn How to Think?...................................99

Chapter 37 — How Do We Create 'Better Thoughts'?.....................103

Chapter 38 — How Lucky People Overcome Difficulties...............107

Chapter 39 — Loneliness as a Strategy in Change.............................111

Chapter 40 — How to Analyze Our Negative Experiences.............115

Chapter 41 — How the Ego Makes People Unlucky. 117

Chapter 42 — The Influence of Our Self-Image in Creating The Future. 119

Chapter 43 — Could Luck Be Based on Belief? 121

Chapter 44 — How Victimization Leads to Self-Sabotage. 123

Chapter 45 — How to Eliminate The Negative Power of the Subconscious Mind. 127

Chapter 46 — The Most Powerful Beliefs. 131

Book Review Request 135

Books Written By The Author 137

Copyright Page

How to Get Lucky: How to Change Your Mind and Get Anything in Life

By Dan Desmarques

Copyright © Dan Desmarques, 2021 (1st Ed.). All Rights Reserved.

Published by 22 Lions Publishing

About

Publisher & Bookstore: 22Lions.com

Author: Biolinky.co/dandesmarques

Introduction.

In history, many were the kings and emperors that seemed to be lucky in moments that were against all odds. They knew something that others would consider speculation, hallucination, or superstition.

There is, however, a science behind their achievements, a science of being lucky.

Those who have used it attracted awards and won competitions. For this reason, many were the scientists that decided to research this phenomenon and discover specific patterns that differentiate the lucky ones from the unlucky ones.

In this book, you will get the exact formula that can make you a lucky person.

This book also offers you several exercises to practice, and that will help you change your mental patterns, so that luck becomes something you naturally attract to your life.

Chapter 1 — The Opportunities You Ignore.

Everything that you see in your life, and how you see your self, is in a perfect correlation.

Your environment shapes you as you also shape the environment.

Most people, however, allow their environment to condition their habits, and that's when they begin — and then often continue forever — to stick to the habits of this same environment.

Have you noticed that most people don't want to change country, return to the country where they were born, and rather die where they were born?

Even the sense of nationality permeates the minds of the majority in the planet.

The vast majority are terrified of being separated from their roots, their family, their childhood friends.

How can you grow, if you insist on living in the past?

Changes demand that you change. You can't be in location B while being in location A.

You can create philosophies and theories about it, you can practice meditation techniques that help you to recenter yourself, you can watch movies about other countries, but the only true change that can ever transform you, and positively, is the one that changes you from the inside — the core of your identity, with its values and beliefs.

This shift of awareness begins with awareness, or the actions you take towards learning about what you want.

- If you want to make more money, for example, you will read about money;

- If you want to learn a specific skill, you find the courses that teach you how to develop that skill.

Many people put barriers at this stage — they will say: 'I have no time!', or 'I have no money to spend!'

These two, among many other excuses, are self-created, but delusional.

Did you know that most online courses — including courses created by famous universities — are free?

Did you know that many books are available for free on the internet?

There is a huge abundance of knowledge that most people ignore. And the most basic and simple way to access that knowledge, is by listening.

When was the last time you went to listen someone speaking about success in life?

When was the last time you downloaded a podcast about how to achieve your goals?

It doesn't matter in which country you are. Everyone has a story of success to tell you, either it occurred in a war, or during the planting of potatoes.

The laws of farming, as the laws of war, fall into the same patters, and these patterns have strategies, thoughts, values, beliefs, etc.

Successful people, either they are entrepreneurs or artists, need to know these things — that's the structure of what we see as marketing, selling, promoting, and most importantly, creating and producing value.

How do you learn how to create a good product, if you don't know which one is more likely to take you towards success?

Many naive people assume that any product will sell if people buy. But that's not how it works.

There is a reason as to why so many people try to sell the same product, but only one, or a few, succeed.

There is a reason why less than 5% of the authors in the world can make a living, even though many write on similar topics.

HOW TO GET LUCKY: HOW TO CHANGE YOUR MIND AND GET ANYTHING IN LIFE

There is a reason as to why some find luck and other don't.

The purpose of this book is to show you the path to that luck, because, in truth, such path is within you.

What I am trying to say here is that, the path towards luck, is different for everyone, albeit the procedure to find it is similar in everyone.

Chapter 2 — The Difference Between Dreamers and Fools.

Once you understand that you are as entitled to be lucky as anyone else, and the only difference is in the efforts you put to understand yourself, and your own personal path of luck, the transformation begins.

You see, it is all about belief.

A person that believes that he can be lucky, will find the opportunities to get lucky, will appreciate them, act on them, and get the results he expects to have.

Those who don't believe in their potential, are miserable. And that's the true source of misery.

I understand that it is difficult to believe in luck when your stomach is empty and your main purpose is to survive. But even Buddha said that one must have a full stomach before meditating.

You must feed yourself, satisfy your basic needs, before you can think about luck. That is why I recommend everyone to first get a job, any job.

Sadly, many people think that by having what they consider "low class jobs" they get further apart from their goal.

That is not true! You won't get closer to being lucky when you are desperate. The vibrations are opposite to one another.

Your mind depends on your vibrations. If you are desperate, you won't attract good ideas, but rather develop desperate and delusional goals.

That's exactly what desperate people do. They say, 'I am going to be very rich', and in the meantime they spend most of their spare time sleeping.

I have met many people like this.

In one case, a security guard with a college degree in History, kept telling me that he would be very rich one day, and then employ me to work for him.

It was pathetic to listen to his ideas, but he truly believed in what he was saying.

Any person who believes he will get richer than me and then employ me to work for him, is most likely delusional, because he can't see I possess more knowledge, too much for that delusional goal to manifest.

Meanwhile, he had no idea I had created and managed many companies, he didn't know I had met many billionaires, and worse, he didn't realize all the opportunities I offered him, and that he wasted by acting obsessively on his foolishness.

There is a big difference between having dreams and being a fool.

The fool, represented in the tarot decks as the man that sings on this way to a cliff, can't see either the barriers or the opportunities surrounding him.

The dreamer is an observer — he sees, acts and is inspired, in a perfect equilibrium between all these three things.

Once I even told that friend that I could create his own business website, when he told me that he was looking for someone to do that for him.

I told him he would pay only for my time, but I would take much less than what he was willing to pay someone else for a low quality result.

I also told him that I would teach him the necessary strategies to promote and sell online.

What did he do? He insulted!

'You just want my money!', he said.

After that moment, I ended the friendship.

I blocked him from social media and forgot about him.

Chapter 3 — How a Belief in Help Shapes Your Attitude.

The vast majority of the people I met, are just too stupid to see the help I provide them.

This isn't even a genuine stupidity, but a deliberate form of ignorance. It comes from selfishness, and a narcissistic attitude towards others. But what is narcissism if not despair in disguise, trying to hide shame?

Most people are too ashamed of themselves to look in the mirror and accept defeat.

The problem is that, if you can't accept defeat, you are not likely to find victory.

Soldiers know that, what prepares them for victory the best, is the intensive training they have on the worse scenarios possible.

Also in life, if you are not prepared to fail, you won't be able to succeed. Because success always follows failures, from which you learn and improve.

Now, if someone can't look at himself as he is, how can he improve? And if he can't improve, how can he make the right decisions that will lead him to success?

You see where I am going? A person must be humble to change.

Most people think they can only reach success by themselves, without any help from someone else. And that's stupid! But it's a deliberate state of ignorance.

Why? Because the book you read and is effective, for example, was created by someone who wants to help you and doesn't even know you.

The interviews you listen, the seminars you attend, the person in the bank that gives you the loan to invest in your business idea, all these people, are helping you.

If you can't believe you must be helped, you won't be helped.

Now let us ponder over this. Lots of people go around thinking that they must steal knowledge from others. A lot of people I meet, try to trick me into giving them answers on how to be successful. And that's humiliating, selfish, self-degrading, pathetic and dumb.

What is my thought on those people? I do what any successful person does. I ignore them. I refuse to help them.

The first thing I do when people want to learn from me, is to offer them a job or a book to read. And all of them reject that!

People want to get rich without working or reading.

They normally want information without experience — by stealing it, getting it resumed in a few minutes.

The result of that is that they lose my friendship, they lose the opportunity, and they learn nothing at the end.

That's their karma!

Everyone that maintains such attitude, goes through life without ever knowing their potential. Their luck departs from them.

My case is just an example. But everything else will be within the same frequency.

The frequency of luck then demands a new attitude — of respect, appreciation, gratitude, and admiration, of willingness to work —, in those who want to be successful.

This attitude begins in how you treat the people you know and the help you receive.

Chapter 4 — The Greatest Fear in Us.

You must want to see yourself as you are, before you can see your other self, as you want it to be.

That demands a combination of both deliberate fantasy, as well as responsibility.

That's what differentiates an adult from a child — the capacity to dream at will, while also being fully responsible for the outcome.

In order to do that, one must overcome his fears.

If we were we as we should be, we wouldn't need to change.

Changes then demand that one recognizes the self from a point in reality beyond that which he calls real.

Such beyond is hidden behind the most frightening, and simultaneously intriguing, veil: the fear of failure — with all other fears that come with it, such as rejection, deception, hurt, and so on.

Any of those fears becomes insignificant once the veil is lifted.

The greatest fear is, therefore, the fear of remaining in the same place. It is the fear of waking up because one has decided to remain asleep.

All dreams are just dreams for those who sleep. And yet, they expect to wake up somewhere else, rather than the place where they decided to sleep.

That's an illusion!

Illusions are then self-imposed to suppress our fears.

We can overcome such fears through our innate will to be curious.

The happiness we gather in our heart, when we are curious about something, and transform the challenge ahead into a game, transforms our being, from wanting to avoid the fear, to actually wanting to face it.

We can do that, when we face its opposite — boredom. The state of remaining in the same place, doing the same things we have been doing for the past years.

Quite often, it is not the courage to move forward, but rather the need to avoid the repetition of the past, the boredom of the present, that propels us to act in the direction ahead of us, and towards accepting new challenges in life.

In this sense, the disgust, discomfort, and even resentment, that we feel for our present condition, shows itself necessary for a positive transformation.

The one who enjoys his life as it is, has no reasons to change. He will reject any opportunity to remove him from where he is.

That is actually what people do, when they find excuses not to do something. That's the most basic reason for procrastination.

That state leads most people, as I saw often, to atheism, over the years.

Habits and routines, repeated for long enough, turn people apathetic, easily manipulated and obedient. And that's what the system, the society as it is, the political body, wants, to maintain itself.

Changes frighten those who don't want them, and that's why everyone will oppose yours.

Chapter 5 — Change as a Natural Necessity.

What is natural is to change! The need to change is a normal and natural need in us, even though we rarely see it.

Why people can't see this? Because they lack excitement in their life.

Your dreams must excite you, make you curious, if you wish to be moved by such energy.

That's how you overcome your present conditions and the fear of change.

Your dreams must be so exciting and inspiring, that you willingly decide to be uncomfortable to pursue them.

You see, that person that wakes up every morning, while others sleep, to run, or work more hours, doesn't do that because he likes it, but because he is inspired.

Inspiration drives us to do things that are uncomfortable, because the goal ahead is more exciting than the benefits of remaining warm in bed for a few more couple of minutes or hours.

If I wish to wake up every morning to do sports, the reason must be so strong, that it excites me, no matter what kind of weather I face when going outside, and no matter if it's a sunny day or still night.

One of the things that confuses people a lot about me, is that they think I was born a writer. They assume that, because they are lazy themselves, some are born with all the talents, and the rest is merely naturally doing their thing, you know, what they call being lucky.

When they realize the amount of books I wrote, and start doing the math at the speed, they then panic.

After that, they assume I am either lying about it, or that I have some kind of mental disorder.

They have to see themselves under the light of being normal, and therefore, they think I am the abnormal one.

Instead of calling themselves stupid and lazy, people prefer to look at those like me as if we are insane, or gifted with some special trick.

Many people I met actually think I steal information or communicate with demons.

I have heard all kind of imbecile comments from those I once respected, which led me to realize that the vast majority of the population is extremely stupid, even though, as mentioned before, stupid by their own choice.

In truth, one must create his own luck if he wishes to have it. He must be willing to do what others won't, if he wants to have what others don't.

What they will call luck, you will see as being outstanding — doing more than anyone else.

Whenever people called me lucky for being a full-time writer, and traveling the world, I used to answer them: "If you can write three hundred books in less than five years; and if you are willing to sacrifice your time, by not partying, not socializing, and even your own health, by sitting all day long in front of a laptop; if you are willing to travel to the poorest countries just to save more money, to write more, in many cases, books that won't sell, you can have the same lifestyle as me."

Nobody likes this answer, because it puts responsibility in the center of the being — at the same level of the dream one has been ignoring.

This centering of responsibility in the self is what scares people the most.

As Sigmund Freud said, "Most people do not really want freedom, because freedom involves responsibility, and most people are afraid of responsibility."

People just wan't to get lucky. But that's an infantile viewpoint on reality!

HOW TO GET LUCKY: HOW TO CHANGE YOUR MIND AND GET ANYTHING IN LIFE

Sure, you may want to get lucky, and you can get lucky, but only if you obey the laws of nature — laws that imply responsibility and action. "We cannot command Nature except by obeying her" (Francis Bacon).

Many of the first people to fly were dreamers, but only those who obeyed the mechanics of life and nature survived their flight.

Others, that thought only about flying, but not landing, weren't so lucky.

Chapter 6 — How the Rich and the Poor Think.

Once you discover which dream excites you the most, and makes you want to get out of the bed in those cold winters, sleep less, and just keep on going, working and working, until you manifest it, the next stage you find is exactly that, the work itself.

I know what you are thinking: "Work more to get lucky?"

Yes, the next stage is to work on your luck. But this work starts in your mind.

I was once in a conversation with a very stupid young man from Ukraine, who told me that you should never strategize or plan, you should just do things.

I asked him: 'How do you do something without thinking and researching first? How do you even learn from your mistakes and correct them if you do not plan?'

He said: 'That's all bullshit! Researching is bullshit! You just do things until you get what you want.'

I answered him: 'Well then, that's why you are an employee in a job you hate, and I'm a business owner traveling the world.'

That's exactly the difference between the moron that thinks he knows more than those who don't need a job, and the person that literally creates his own income.

Successful people don't think like that! In fact, all the business owners I met admire me.

Some say I am courageous, for investing in businesses that are more likely to fail. Others say that I have the gift to attract money from the air, because I literally create books from my head and other businesses out of my ideas only.

In other words, I don't need other resources for my creations besides my own mind, as, for example, the owner of some factory or restaurant.

It is actually interesting that I always and easily make friends with business owners, but it's the stupid of society, the miserable, that think they are smarter than me and then insult me and my beliefs.

In reality, I have to be courageous and creative to do what I do and succeed. But for the losers of this world, I am the idiot.

That's why they will never have my lifestyle.

My work started far before I decided to become a writer. I had to first work on myself, at that point in time, only acquiring knowledge, but also changing my views on life.

I never ceased doing this type of work. Because we are constantly facing morons and other low quality people, that want to change our thinking patterns and our values.

We need to protect our thoughts and reinforce our mind, if we wish to achieve our goals.

Our mind is the most valuable asset we have.

Unfortunately, that also demands being selective with the people you surround yourself with.

As the majority are garbage, full of jealousy and hatred for those who accomplish what they can't do themselves, and won't do as well, due to laziness and apathy, you will spend a lot of your time alone, dreaming and working on your dreams.

Leaders and successful business owners are lonely people, not by choice, but due to the lack of it.

It is much easier to succeed when you have the love, attention and support of many — when you have a reason and a purpose beyond yourself.

HOW TO GET LUCKY: HOW TO CHANGE YOUR MIND AND GET ANYTHING IN LIFE

It may be hard at first, and in my situation, I still feel it's hard after all these years, but I simply accept this condition as the only possible, and take advantage of the situation the best I can. I do that by traveling more and enjoying my life, and the money I earn.

Chapter 7 — Why I Travel So Much.

One thing people often notice wrongly about me, is that they see me a traveler.

They think I travel because I like to travel, and don't want to stay anywhere.

They think I will never like any country or city, and therefore will travel all my life.

They see the world through dichotomies, and always assume that, when something isn't one thing, it must be the opposite.

They lack the capacity to think beyond simple dualities.

It is as if they only knew two numbers: One plus one is two, and when two is subtracted by one, is one. And that's it! They ignore all the other numbers.

I travel a lot but I don't see myself as a traveler. I am simply restless.

I don't succumb to apathy as the majority of the population.

Most people are so apathetic, that they see apathy as normal. They think that someone that travels a lot and constantly, must have some problem to solve, or is running away from something.

In fact, when the coronavirus forced them to stay at home, many were quite happy about it. Rather than having to move to work, they could now just spend their whole life inside a small box called home.

I just can't imagine a life like that!

The reason why I travel so much, is because most people I encounter are useless as potential friends — selfish, entitled, lazy and too slow.

The vast majority of the people only go out once a month, if ever, to talk to others.

They are not interested in making friends, or in doing outdoor activities, especially in European countries.

That's why I leave their country! I get bored with them! They are too lazy and numb.

Their life goes nowhere, and they slowdown mine.

Because they move slowly in life, the conversations are always the same, the questions are always the same, and the expectations are always the same. And because they have nothing to else do, and rather spend their time at home, they don't have much to speak, except movies and gossip.

Traveling is the only way I have of keeping my sanity at the same level of my efforts.

It's too hard to work so much and then try to balance your lifestyle with the lifestyle of others.

You do better by traveling, enjoying your money, and spoiling yourself with the result of your accomplishments and efforts.

In fact, using your money on yourself, will motivate you to keep doing more of what you are already doing.

That is why, when you dream, you must dream not only about what kind of life you want to have, but also about what you can accomplish once your dreams are fulfilled.

Chapter 8 — Using Your Dreams to Motivate You.

In the past, I had a girlfriend that owned a business but hated her business.

She was always telling me that she didn't like what she was doing, which was to meet with clients, sell them security doors, and so on.

To motivate her, I said: 'But you like to travel, don't you? And you like to explore different cities, rather than being stuck in one single country, right? So, you do that to enjoy the lifestyle you want to have, and one day maybe you get a better idea on how to make money.'

Once she started connecting traveling with her work, she started getting better ideas, enjoying more, and also making more money, which then allowed her to travel more.

I also taught her how to make business plans, which definitely taught her the importance of strategizing and correcting herself.

Before meeting me, she didn't believe in any of those things.

She never planned. She was completely dependent on randomness. And obviously, she saw herself as unlucky too. She was struggling to make money.

When you dream about what you want, it is important that you are explicit about the benefits it has for you. You must dream also about what you can do with what you want to get.

If you want more money, where will you use it?

What will you do?

Will you help someone in need with that money?

Who will benefit from your money besides you?

Who will you help?

Do you see where I am going?

Money is a flow of energy, that is then transferred to its material form, which we use to make transactions.

Money in itself is not real. And neither is our concept of value. Everything is in our head.

What for some people is perfect, for others is madness.

I love to have the freedom to travel and go where I want, when I want, for example, but for the vast majority of the people I meet, that is madness.

They think what is normal is to stay somewhere for many years.

People are constantly trying to pin me somewhere, as if I was some tree.

It messes with their head, the idea that I can just go where I want.

This is particularly true with women. They think, 'oh, you can just leave me?'

People have an extremely poor view of their world. They think in terms of owning and controlling.

Seems like nobody trusts honesty anymore. It's all about, 'what can I get and for how long?'

I think most people have this idea that they will live forever, because they don't seem interested in doing anything else besides maintaining their routines social status quo.

I find that extremely boring and depressive. But they think it is normal.

Chapter 9 — What is Money for You?

They way people look at the world, and money, is usually not very different.

Those who pin themselves to some land, tend to assume money is scarce, and that they must get it by climbing the social ladder.

Only the ones who see the opportunities all over the world, find themselves dreaming more than the common person, and also seeing more ways of spending money.

You are never so rich that you can't easily spend all of your money in things that make you happy.

One of my favorite hobbies when I was in China, was to buy toys for poor children. It gave me joy to make more money, and then use it to buy toys for kids, and see them smile.

Whatsoever is the reason why you want to make more money, make sure it changes your emotions and how you see yourself. Because it will help you change your view on money.

If you want to have a certain job or business, imagine what you can do with it, the people you can employ, the projects you can do with that business.

You see, when you have more money, you can buy employees, you can buy businesses, software, and you can help really a lot of people that also need it, but can't get it in the same way you do.

Create a network of possibilities, of 'whys' when dreaming. Make a list of, at least four things, you will do with your money, and everything else you will get as a result.

- Who will you help if you start receiving more money?

- How will you help others if you have more money?

- Which lifestyle do you want to have, if you suddenly make double of what you have now?

- Where you will want to live if you make more money? In which country? With what kind of weather?

Once you have the answer to the questions above, close your eyes, and imagine all those things. Not just the having of such things, but the doing — what will you do and who will you be with such things?

Remember what I said previously about having a dream that excites you so much, that you don't care about the cold, the working hours, and the place where you work?

Well, now consider having a dream that, apart from these things, also excites you in regard to the new opportunities and possibilities.

- What will you buy with more money for yourself and others?

- With whom do you want to live once you gain a new lifestyle?

- Where do you want to get married?

- What kind of people do you want to have near you?

Make your vision and opportunities as exciting as your goals!

Chapter 10 — How to Change the Synapses in Your Brain.

If it feels difficult to imagine yourself living your dream, write it down first, and then read.

Write about it every day if you have to, until visualizing the dream becomes easy and natural.

Get a notebook, and write every morning about that dream.

Do you know what you can also do? Surprise yourself!

Write notes and letters to yourself. Put them in your mailbox, and then pick them up in another day. Or create an alert message in your smartphone, that says: 'Your dream is coming!'

Be creative with what you want to have, in order to change the synapses of your brain.

Our synapses are made out of habits — the things we consistently do, speak and remember.

If you are able to orient your mind, towards thinking new thoughts and imagining new things, those mental patterns will change, and gradually, imagining yourself getting what you want, will seem more and more natural to you.

It is also important that you repeat to yourself mantras.

By mantras, I mean phrases that help you reprogram your mind.

Those phrases don't have to be in Hindu or any other Asian language; only your own language.

You can choose any mantras.

The purpose of the mantras is to reinforce your belief system.

Here are some examples:

- 'I deserve to get what I want to get';
- 'Money is coming effortlessly and easily to my life';
- 'What I dream, is coming to me with God's blessing';
- 'I will get what I want to have because that's the law of vibration'.

There is no specific amount of times needed to precisely repeat the mantras, but you can choose a number yourself, that keeps you for at least thirty minutes a day repeating them.

The more you repeat such mantras, the better.

Do it while showering, for example. As it's something you do every day, it becomes a new routine in your life, that will then simply keep your mind under the right frequency.

Meanwhile, it is important that you know that many things you want won't come directly to you, but rather indirectly. Reason why it's important that you put equal efforts to enjoy your life as much as you can.

Check for opportunities to visit theaters, museums, and parks in your area, and allow that constant change of environment to inspire you.

If you meet someone knew — and I have met lots of people when on my own, while exploring cities — remember that this person may give you the exact message that you need. So make sure you spend some time getting to know that person.

Chapter 11 — How to Find The People You Need in Life.

I am often asked how do I get so many girlfriends so easily, but that's not really a purpose of mine.

As a matter of fact, I rather have one stable relationship. That's what I truly seek!

The reason why that happens, is that I spend so much time alone, in front of my laptop, that I always remain open to meeting new people, and quite often, I do.

I usually end up having long conversations with people I never expected to encounter. And that's how I find beautiful women I never expected to meet.

The failure in those relationships isn't so much within my reach.

You see, other people don't think like what I am explaining in this book, so they have a different attitude to life.

They can't see beyond their immediate reach and what their eyes can observe. And for them, that's all that reality is.

They see very little with their eyes.

They have no sense of spiritual awareness or purpose.

For most women, I am not normal. And they are always afraid to be abandoned. So they themselves destroy the relationship, in order to test that fear, which is stupid, for it makes it real.

You don't test how hard a cup of class is, by throwing it at a wall;

You don't test how strong you are by hitting your head against a wall;

And you shouldn't test the strength of a relationship by damaging it.

But that's exactly what women do.

That's why I am still single, despite the many relationships I had.

That, I would say, is the price to pay for doing what others don't. You will hit the exact target in all these fears. And you can't waste your life thinking about theirs.

It won't work like that!

Even if doing that could work, it will be too late to even consider it.

I remember once I was dating a beautiful Belarusian girl when living in Poland. I really liked her a lot. But she started getting paranoid fears, about being abandoned, or that I could be some criminal escaping justice, and not just a traveler, that I lied about being a writer, and so on.

She started picking fights and then vanished.

I tried to contact her by any means I could, and even sent flowers to her office.

She never said anything. So I moved on with my life.

Nearly five months later, she sent me a message, apologizing for her behavior, and asking for another chance to talk to me.

I received that message one day before leaving Poland, when I had everything packed and ready to travel to another country.

Five months is a lot of time for me. But for most people is nothing. It's the same as one or two days.

As mentioned previously, most people have a very poor concept of time. They don't have any sense of urgency. And they are also not good at judging the people who enter their life.

I did the only thing I could do in that situation, which was to ignore her, and just move on.

I also still get messages from a girlfriend I had in Lithuania, two years ago.

HOW TO GET LUCKY: HOW TO CHANGE YOUR MIND AND GET ANYTHING IN LIFE

Again, she can't really perceive the gravity of her actions, or the implications they have.

Maybe she even expects me to forget cheating, if it occurred years ago.

Chapter 12 — People Have a Short Memory.

It is because people have this fish-like brain, and analyze life like some dumb fish in a lake, that trying to understand them, becomes a complete waste of years of our life.

It doesn't even matter how nice you are to someone. If that person can't see life as you see it, she or he, will destroy whatever you do, and confuse everything you say.

People who don't believe in help, for example, typically see all forms of help as an attack, an attempt at manipulating them.

Those who see life as a struggle for survival, in which everyone is for himself, won't understand the meaning of being helped or doing things together as a team.

Logic doesn't work with most people.

You can't explain them their emotions, and convince them into having different emotions or different thoughts.

They will always prioritize their lack of reason to justify their emotions.

Once I realized that — and it took me nearly 40 years to accept it — I stopped suffering because of what others do.

'You think I am crazy, and obsessed with money and work? Fine! Pack your stuff and get out of the house. You can't pay it anyway' I said to my last girlfriend in Croatia.

Does this seem ruthless and cold hearted to you?

It is isn't, I can assure you. It all depends in the priorities you have in life.

As I told her, 'It's not that I don't love you, but rather that I love myself and my life too much, to allow you to destroy what I built'.

If a plane drops its oxygen masks during an emergency, you are told to put the mask first on yourself, as you can't help anyone else if you are unconscious.

If someone is drowning, you need to make sure you can actually help that person, as you won't help anyone by drowning along with the person.

Instinct makes people do exactly the opposite of what I just said.

Movies and fairytales constantly tell us that sacrifice is noble and a true demonstration of love. So people believe that this is the meaning of life — to have drama, sacrifice, cry and play into conflicts.

How much do you think you will accomplish if you are too busy solving conflicts?

Which one is easier: To work while happy, or to focus on your work while sharing the space with people you hate?

Do your dreams include quarrels and disagreements?

If that is how you see your ideal lifestyle, please go ahead, and dream conflicts into existence.

If that is not how you see yourself living your ideal life, then don't allow anyone to disrespect you.

Learn to let the imbecile go and depart from your dream.

Not everyone wants to be happy. Many people are as afraid to be happy as they are afraid to be responsible for their conflicts and problems. They will attack efforts to make them happy.

To love someone is then to know whom you can't love. "A person has to be willing to have and willing to lose before he can completely be. He must be willing to hate and be hated, leave and be left before he can love" (L. Ron Hubbard).

Chapter 13 — The Influence of Time and Space.

We don't know exactly how long it takes to get something we envision, to change the outcome of our life, and that's why it's important to cultivate patience.

I've noticed that the most lazy people are also, interestingly, the most impatient. And how can you have something that you don't work for, if you are not even patient enough to compensate for that same laziness?

You see, faith and hard work are related — one works the most, for that which he believes with a stronger conviction.

It is then important that a person envisions every day, without giving up, no matter how many months, or years it takes, to get what we want.

I had experiences in my life, in which I truly felt like giving up. My life was going nowhere, I had no reasons to trust my goals would ever be achieved. But I created a routine, of going every day to an empty church, close my eyes there, and envision myself with what I wanted to have.

Another thing I did, was, every night and every morning, imagine myself with what I wanted to have.

I never considered the hypothesis of never having it. I did not even consider having it.

I simply imagined myself as if I was there. I saw it as a way to compensate for the life I didn't like.

I poured my emotions into those dreams. And those dreams, at that time, was all I had.

After that, everything started to unfold.

In about a few months, I got a job offer to another country, which I accepted. And after that, once I arrived, I saw everything I wished before coming to reality.

You see, my dream did not manifest where I was. I had to be removed from that place first, before I could get what I wanted.

Most people don't realize that the place where they live may not be the ideal to manifest their dreams. And that's why many opportunities appear for them to travel, to be removed from where they are. And yet, many reject those opportunities, because they think such opportunities aren't related to their dreams.

They want to go from A to C without having to experience B.

The law of miracles doesn't work that way.

If your location is not ideal for your personal transformation, many other things will occur first, before your dreams manifest.

That may imply meeting the man or woman of your life, the job you always wanted to have, the house where you always wanted to live, and other things, far from where you though you would have them.

Chapter 14 — How Karma Attracts the Right People.

Another thing I realized, is that many times, people enter our life to show us things that, otherwise, we would never see on our own.

I have visited many countries that I never considered visiting, because of a relationship I had.

Now, the relationship wasn't going well, and eventually ended. But that person had to enter my life to show me things I wasn't even considering in my mind. Things that made a huge difference in my path.

Once I became more independent, her path went in another direction. And likewise, she also did not consider that she was being removed from my life by herself, with her own opinion.

She simply met another man during one of our fights, when we were apart.

She eventually regretted what she did, but it was too late.

The truth is, we also lose what we gain, in order to learn to value the things or people we once had.

The two states — gratitude and opportunity — are correlated.

You must appreciate what you have because it's what leads you where you want to be, even, and including, in situations where you aren't as happy as you wish you were.

I have noticed that better people always come to our reality, when we are ready to move on to better places. But we are usually afraid to lose what we have, and we want to make the things we had, or the relationships that are failing, work, and then we lose it all — the relationship we had and the opportunities ahead of us.

Every moment of our life, shows a lot more than what we can see.

I wouldn't move to Croatia, and then stay in Croatia, if I didn't met a Croatian woman that I believed was the type of woman I was looking for.

Once we started living together, she changed, or at least, allowed the mask to fall, and I saw a repetition of my past coming to my life again.

I had to end the relationship when she started getting abusive and disrespectful. And yet, here I was, in Zagreb, in a big apartment near the river, by myself.

For what? Most likely, to finish my books.

Everything that has been happening in my life for the past months, is forcing me in this direction.

I will know why once this period is over. For now, all I can do, is to accept these changes and appreciate the results.

I don't have time to mourn failed relationships, and I had too many in 2020.

I can't change other people, or expect them to be someone they will never be, because they can't see what I see. I can only be me.

Also interesting, is that since I arrived in Zagreb, I have experienced dozens of earthquakes.

Each earthquake, during my sleep, or when I work, shows me that life is fragile, and can end at any moment.

Such awareness, pushes me to keep going, even when I am exhausted.

I started drinking more healthy juices to increase my energy level.

So, as you see, all these things happened, just because I met one Croatian woman whom I thought was the woman I was looking for.

The illusion brought me somewhere else, to experience something I never would experience otherwise.

If I didn't meet her, I would certainly not even visit Zagreb. My plan was to go somewhere else at the time we met.

Chapter 15 — Bad Experiences Can Lead to Positive Results.

If someone had told me I would be stuck in Zagreb experiencing earthquakes, and working at home every day, because it was too difficult to make new friends, I would probably never come. I was motivated by other interests — a beautiful woman, a relationship, and sex.

The other experiences in my life, that showed me what I had to learn, weren't that different.

I moved to certain cities because I didn't like others.

I moved to certain countries, because I had a good job offer.

One thing is all that is necessary, for us to experience the rest. And the rest is what matters. But it is beyond our control.

You see, you can't get luck directly. What you get are the opportunities to get lucky.

Those opportunities come to you, when you allow yourself to move with the flow, that flow of luck.

Luck is like a rubber duck floating in a wave. You need to allow yourself to enter the stormy sea, to get the rubber duck. And if you find yourself in a beautiful island, because you chased a rubber duck, during a moment of stormy waters, that is your luck.

The many people that you hate, but enter your life to disrupt it, are part of that stormy sea.

Many times, you think they are taking the rubber ducks away from you, and even they themselves may believe that, but as everything is connected, they end up putting you where you should be.

If it wasn't for my enemies, I wouldn't get better and better jobs.

Every time I lost one, because of false rumors, I would get a better one somewhere else, in a better city, with a higher salary.

The ones who are disloyal, wicked and perverted, have only themselves as their own support.

It is the evil, fearful and disgusting that support similar people. But those who have God, have everything they need.

I have been abandoned by many people I trusted in times of need. But God never abandoned me.

That is why, instead of trying to keep many friends and good relations with my awful family, I decided to be more moral and a better servant of God.

That is how my life became what others call "lucky".

Wherever I go, people say I'm lucky.

I'm not lucky because I work a lot for what I have.

That luck, can all be attributed to a devotion, trust and faith in God.

Chapter 16 — You Won't Find God in a Religious Group.

Quite a lot of people look at life as a competition. They think that in order to get something, they must take it from somewhere else.

Many people I encounter think the same in relation to me. They think they must steal from me what I know. And so, they try to trick me into conversations and false friendships, which invariably, always lead to this attempt.

They trick me into revealing what I know, because they think they must steal it.

It happens often that I believe to be in a normal conversation with a friend, and suddenly, that person finds herself in an ideal spot, like a snake that has trapped me in my own empathy and willingness to help others, persisting then on asking me very private questions, to take as much as possible.

Once I reveal to those people what I know, they vanish, and I never hear from them again.

If I send them a message, they won't even reply me.

Quite a lot of people are extremely selfish and manipulative. They see the world in that way, that someone else has what they want, and they must take it from that person.

That decadent way of looking at the world, is anti-God, and far more common than I would expect, even among christians and other religious groups.

In fact, what I described above, happened to me with many religious people that I have met in different countries.

Those who were not interested in stealing from me, were often leading me into conversations in which I should, supposedly, admit that I stole what I know from someone else.

They wanted to know where I got my knowledge, from whom or which group I took it from.

They would even follow my social accounts to withdraw as much information as they could in that sense.

It's really disgusting, to see Freemasons, Rosicrucians, Scientologists, Jehovah Witnesses, and many, really many, other groups, doing this. But I saw it so often, I can now clearly say: that is what they are and what they represent.

Religion now is just an empty hole full of snakes. There is nothing there but disappointment and evil thoughts.

God is in none of the religions of this world. Reason why, I am convinced the church of God is within those who follow these words, and trust, with faith, that everything is given to them if they trust God.

Chapter 17 — God's Kingdom is Within You.

There is no such thing as competition in the kingdom of God. God doesn't obey the material laws of scarcity and math.

The science of God is the science of miracles. He makes the impossible possible. And that's why nobody, who is not orientated by God, will ever understand who I am.

They will hate me, because their god is Satan.

Readers who pray for answers, always find my books. And why is that? Why do people who pray for the truth, find my books? Because their prayers and my books are part of the same kingdom.

If you ever caught yourself thinking that someone else has your money, someone else has what you want, and if you don't get something, is because you must steal it, take it from somewhere else, fake a friendship to meet a successful man or woman, remember my words: those are the thoughts of a narcissistic and satanic mindset.

If you wish to attract luck through God, you must ignore the idea that what you want is being taken by someone.

God doesn't work with material laws. He is within the idea of unlimited abundance. Because He, Himself, is unlimited.

Any thought that compares your achievements with another human being, or makes you assume you must take what you want from someone, departs you from the Divine Light that guides you towards any of your dreams.

Always trust that you can get the most absurd things, because they are indeed possible.

One of the things I wrote once in a piece of paper, is that I didn't want to pay rent anymore. I wanted to get a free house.

I never knew that would even be possible. I simply wrote it, because I wanted it. And well, when I got my first job offer in China, they said I didn't have to pay rent for the apartment.

In fact, during the years I lived in China, I was hosted in beautiful hotel apartments, with furniture and kitchen, and cleaning maids that would come once a week, and I never had to pay anything for all of that.

Some of my friends said I simply got lucky. Yes, but I also wrote that in a piece of paper, and I never thought it would be possible to get it. I had no idea.

Theories don't matter in this case. It doesn't matter if I channeled the information from somewhere else, if some spirit of a dead person whispered in my hears, or if I crossed into a parallel reality. All that matters is that I got what I wanted. And that accomplishment, comes from faith.

I applied the same faith to write more than 300 books. I told God this is what I wanted. I wanted to serve him.

Chapter 18 — With God Everything is Possible.

Most people surely would say it's not humanely possible for one person to possess so much information as I do.

Many of my readers wondered the same, and asked me how can I have so much knowledge about so many things, and be right on so many things as well.

That's just not possible! And yes, they are right, it's not possible to a normal human being.

What God did, was open all these doors of my mind and spirit, unblocking my conscience, often during my sleep, as the mind offers the least resistance during these periods, to let me see my past lives.

A lot of knowledge was also poured into my mind during these periods. I used to wake up full of headaches, as if someone had forced a whole library into my head.

I spent many years like that, having dreams of my lives in other planets, getting entire libraries of knowledge into my head, and this happened so often, that now I can say that I do have more knowledge than most people on the planet.

Again, it is not normal for a human being to have so much knowledge. I got that from God. And that is how I was able to write 300 books.

Why 300? Because I only have one body.

I have so much knowledge, that I can easily write over three thousand books, and break all the records for the most amount of books ever written.

I often write a whole book in one day, or less than 24 hours, as it is the case of the book you are reading right now. And I can do it easily, because this knowledge, everything you are reading here, was already in my mind. I simply had to take the time to write it.

Now, when I said to God I wanted to write more than 300 books, I didn't know that would be possible. I found the answers later.

I know it is possible now, but I didn't know I could do it when I wished for it.

So, as you see, thinking about what you can or can't do, is useless. For God, all that matters is your faith.

Others will say you are lucky, because they are blind.

Luck is a word used by blind people without faith.

I used it for the purpose of this book, because I know this is what many interpret as realistic. But the true power of luck is attributed by God.

Chapter 19 — How to Communicate With God.

In order to communicate to God what you want, you must see yourself having it.

Your imagination must be so real, that it will look like a memory of something that has already happened before. So much so, that when you get it, it will seem like a repetition of the past.

As a matter of fact, the reason why we keep repeating the same experiences of the past, is because we keep giving energy to our memories.

When you keep remembering that relationship that ended, and you resent that person, you drive hate and other forms of energy to those memories, and you then attract a similar person.

The same applies to our problems and challenges.

So what do you want to attract? You want to attract something different from your past — which means not repeating the same memories.

That implies having new memories. But how can you have new memories to replace old memories, if you keep giving energy to the same memories, and those memories bring more of the same?

Well, that's when imagination comes in. You see, imagining is creating new memories.

Children do this naturally, because they play to develop their mind.

As adults, our mind is already developed. That's the meaning of being an adult — believing and having a whole set of brainwave patterns related to those beliefs. And we become very serious about it. We are absolutely convinced that we are right about everything we know.

A lot of people have this arrogance in them, of assuming that what they know is the whole truth. And then they continue through life by perpetuating this same truth, by keeping themselves attached to it, and replicating it as they go along.

The problem is that, if you want to change your future, and make it into something else, different from where you are going, you must reject this idea that you are a product of fate, or that luck is hidden in some point outside your own control.

In essence, if you want to be lucky, you must put the point of control over luck inside of you.

You do that, by getting the control over your mind.

This control is exercised through the act of imagining the realities you want to live.

In doing that, the patterns in your mind change, the memories of the past fade away, and your reality becomes something else, different from what you were envisioning before.

Have you noticed that when you come back from a long travel to the countryside, or some other city, in another country, you now look at everyone around you and your home in a different light?

That mental state maintains for a few days, until you return to your old habits.

That's exactly what I mean by imagining a new reality and changing your viewpoint. When you look at yourself from the eyes of the observer, the one in the future, you will see yourself in a very different way.

Do this exercise for a moment: Close your eyes, and tell me what kind of person you would want to be, in ten years from now — describe it!

Afterwards, put your mind inside that other you, in the future, and tell me what would he say to you.

Imagine you are both having a conversation, and that now, you are telling me what future-you is saying about present-you.

HOW TO GET LUCKY: HOW TO CHANGE YOUR MIND AND GET ANYTHING IN LIFE

I bet he would say something like: "Oh, well, you made the wrong decision about x, y and z, because you still need to learn this and that. And if you persist, and have faith, you will eventually realize A, B and C, and that's when you become aware that D, E and F are also present. From that point onward, you will find G, H and I."

Now, if you keep doing this exercise often — and I know it sounds totally schizophrenic —, you will eventually gain a wider awareness over your present condition, coming from that other you — your own master within your true self. Because, you see, who you are now, is not the real you.

You are the other you, in the future. You are the person you want to become, and not the one you are now. So that master-you in the future is the real you.

We can call it consciousness, guiding spirit, but whatever it is, is the real you.

Even if you consider that other you to exist already, in another reality, you are still brining that other reality towards you. You are crossing worlds and into the world you want to experience. Because, truly, you are whom you want to become.

If you are not still that individual, it is only because you have chosen to neglect the opportunity.

That opportunity, as I am showing you, is present in you.

Chapter 20 — The Greatest Secret About Luck.

The greatest secret about luck, is that we own it.

We owe to ourselves to create our own luck. The limit is only our imagination. And we increase this limit, by exercising the imagination.

The amount of weights that a weightlifter can lift, is determined by his practice, as much as your life is determined by your imagination.

Whatever you can see in your mind, you can have in your hands. That is the law of this universe. You must have what you see, or as Freud said, succumb to accept what you have, when you can't see more than that.

The fate of those that can't get more from life, is determined by their lack of faith.

Faith and fate are then related only to the amount of energy one pours in either his memories or his imagination.

If your imagination is strong enough, your fate becomes what others will call 'luck'.

Once we become the observation, the observation will then look at the observer, as just a memory of the past.

Think about it! How much have you changed since you were five years old?

Could you imagine anything of what you have now?

If the answer is yes, then you probably have lived your entire life on default rather than determination.

Many of us have too many dreams that we allow to die. And the richest place on earth is the graveyard, for it is filled with unfulfilled dreams.

Could you imagine yourself talking about your achievements to your friends before you actually got there?

It is as real to consider that from the point of view of your childhood, as it is now to consider it from a point in the future.

Close your eyes, choose a couple of people you know, and imagine yourself telling them about your achievements, posting photos about it on social media, and so on.

In fact, cut images from magazines and put your own photo on top of what you want.

Place this board somewhere in your house.

You can do the same in your computer. It's called your dream-canva.

You can create a canva about anything you want.

This vision board will then help you in imagining the things you want.

When using your imagination, don't just make it static. Be like a child. Imagine yourself having a conversation with someone, moving towards the car of your dream, talking about it, driving it.

If it's a spouse, imagine yourself walking with that person outside, and meeting your friends and family with that person.

You must project scenarios that are realistic, so that those scenarios can become as strong as a memory.

That 'imaginary-memory' is what drives the energy of such reality towards you.

Nobody ever loses anything when applying this law. It is a Devine law, and therefore, constructive. Reason why, when someone tells me they dream about having my lifestyle, I know there is a reason for them to tell me that.

HOW TO GET LUCKY: HOW TO CHANGE YOUR MIND AND GET ANYTHING IN LIFE

Quite often, the reason is that I have one of the gateways to their dream. And I have it because they can help me achieve my own dreams. So, the next thing I do, is consider the why. Why are they telling me that? What can they do for me that will make both of us very rich?

I immediately realize the why, every single time. And guess what happens next?

They abandon the opportunity I give them, because it consists of a lot of work without money.

I gave an opportunity to a friend, to work with me in finding people to publish their book. I offered her 50% from the earnings. But she said it was too difficult to find such people, and quit.

I offered an opportunity to a friend, to create audiobooks for me, as he can speak many languages. He said he didn't want to work without any salary, even if I offered him 50% of the earnings — that's 50% of all the profit ever made, which means he would have a passive income for life on all my audiobooks. He refused!

I told a cousin he could create a business with honey, which I would then use with my Chinese friends to export it to China. All he had to do was start it. I already had the chain of clients ready, as well as the import company to help us. He didn't do it.

You see, people are attracted to me, when they want something that will make both of us rich. But they have a scarcity mentality. They think they must use me, or steal knowledge from me, they think luck comes without action or hard work, and that's how they lose all the opportunities.

I could tell you many hundreds of similar stories, because now that I understand this law, I can clearly see how everyone loses the amazing opportunities coming to their life.

Chapter 21 — Everyone Attracts Luck.

Everyone attracts luck, in abundance, but they can't see it, because they are blind, blind by selfishness, egotism and arrogance.

This idea, that you must steal from someone, and you must do everything alone, and nobody will ever help you, and others just want to use you, and you need money to make money, all these dumb ideas, keep people miserable.

What can I do with them? Nothing! They end up all wasting my time. Because I have to listen to them talking about their dreams, dreams they will never do anything about.

They want to start by the end, by having, without taking any step whatsoever towards the responsibility of working for it. And that's why they lose it.

God doesn't just give what you want, without testing you. God will test your faith first, and before giving you anything. If you fail the test, you won't get anything.

God needs to test your faith to know its real meaning and value. And well, all the christians I ever met, failed this test, because they are arrogant, selfish, and self-absorbed.

I knew a christian speaker that asked me many questions about how to get a life like mine. And again, I saw the why. So I gave him the opportunity: Create a podcast and youtube channel about spirituality, in which we both talk openly.

This would increase my book sales, and give him what he wanted — fame, credibility and popularity as a speaker, and a passive income doing that.

Did he do it? No! Because he wanted the attention on himself only.

He didn't want his followers to know about me, he didn't want 'his people' to know I exist, because I don't belong to his congregation. And therefore, he was afraid I would deviate his people from their faith, and towards my books and my knowledge.

That's arrogance, selfishness, and delusional beliefs within one single person.

I don't care how much people love him. God hates him and despises him.

His conversation with me was how God tested him. He failed!

Where is he now? Where he was — with 40 years old, living on the charity of others from his congregation, without a proper salary or house of his own.

That's the fate of the imbecile that think they are superior to others because their religion is better than the religion of someone else. And that's what I saw in every single religious member.

Indeed, there is no better test to a person of faith, that forcing that person to cooperate with someone else, that doesn't belong to his own community.

That's the ultimate test, when you can communicate and cooperate with someone that may have different views on spirituality.

So you see, God offers gifts to everyone that prays. People lose those gifts because of their imbecility.

God doesn't abandon them. He simply doesn't waste his time on them.

I invited another religious person, who asked me for help in her music career, to spend time with me, work with me, in exchange for that knowledge. I desperately needed an assistant and couldn't find one during the time she wanted those answers.

I told her that she could work with me and in exchange I would give her a whole strategy and plan for her music career.

She didn't do it. Instead, moved to Africa, because some religious leader there said he would publish the music they would create.

Where will she go from there? Nowhere!

Again, she did the same mistake of everyone else. She trusted only a person from her own congregation.

HOW TO GET LUCKY: HOW TO CHANGE YOUR MIND AND GET ANYTHING IN LIFE

Sure, she can be happy, and think she got what she wanted, but that's as happy as a whale in some aquarium.

You could have the whole ocean, and yet, you choose the aquarium, because it makes you feel safe.

Those who put safety above commitment deserve nothing, and get nothing back.

She will experience plenty of loneliness in her life, until she realizes this lesson, if she ever will.

I think most people put way too many efforts in running away from the lessons God asks from them.

They pray and pray, and God shows them the path, and they say: 'Yeah, thanks, but I will keep on waiting for a path that suits me better, because that one doesn't match my egotistic view on life.'

I find most religious people very pathetic. But I have nothing against religion. In fact, I say this because I think they are offensive to God. They don't respect His laws.

Chapter 22 — You Can Change What Others Think of You.

You can increase the magnetism of your projections and imaginary visualizations, by adding an element that you bring with you.

For example, pick a stone, or some other object, put it in front of you, and now imagine looking at it when visualizing your goal.

Can you imagine opening your hand with it, when being with your future spouse, or in front of your favorite car?

When you are able to put an object inside your dream, it is like bridging your goals with the use of that tridimensional object. It becomes easier.

That object can also be a sweater or something else.

Your thoughts have power, and if you project an image of an imaginary object into your environment, it is possible that others will see it too.

Have you every tried doing that?

Here's an exercise for you to try with friends or a spouse: Think of an object, any object, or a goal, that you want them to perceive, but don't tell them you are doing this exercise.

It can be, for example, what you would like to eat. Think of a pizza, and keep that thought in your mind. Keep imagining yourself eating pizza.

Then, wait to see what happens. It's possible that the person in front of you will suggest that both of you go eat pizza.

If you think that was luck or coincidence, keep repeating the same exercise with the same person and with other people.

This is a great way to notice how powerful your thoughts are, and gain more confident when imagining something.

Imagine how powerful you can be, when you are able to change how others see you.

You can literally make them think whatever you want, by holding on to the thoughts you want them to have about yourself.

People can only see what you allow them to see.

The ones who can't see you as you are, will move away from your life, while the people who see you as you want to be seen, will want to be part of your life.

Every time I change, I see the people around me vanishing. I become someone they can't understand. But they did understand me before, when we met. Because, at that point, I was projecting what they wished to see.

Now, consider doing the same exercise to make people praise you, love you, and give you opportunities to make more money, and you will see those things manifesting.

Quite a lot of what happens in our life is attracted foremost by our aura, our perceptions, and our self-image. Rich people are confident, they are confident that the world will give them everything they need.

It is very difficult to become rich without that confidence.

If you think you don't deserve to be rich, even when the opportunities come to you, you will find a way to push them apart.

To believe that you deserve what you want to get, is crucial in the process of attracting it.

Chapter 23 — How to Control Your Mind.

Equally important to putting your focus in what you want to achieve, is the ability to disregard everything you don't want to have.

It is difficult to stop thinking about the things you don't want to think about.

In fact, just as you improve your ability to think more strongly about the things you want to have, it is only natural that the memories and fears related to what you don't want to have, will also become more preeminent in your mind.

The way to deal with those thoughts is to ignore them, and you do that by focusing on other thoughts.

In other words, you don't fight your thoughts. You simple ignore them. And the best way to ignore your thoughts, is to replace them with better thoughts.

The buddhist monks have wonderful way to help people do that — it's called physical work.

It's hard to think when you are working with your body. And surely enough, physical exercise will also help you in dealing with the thoughts you don't want to have.

Quite often, when I ended relationships, that was the only thing I could do to stop thinking about the same person. I would run, sometimes, as often as three times a day.

It didn't matter how long or how far I would run.

You are not preparing yourself for a marathon, but fighting your mind; not being against it, but for it. This is a fight for control.

You don't want your mind to control you. You want to be the one controlling it.

Most people don't know the difference because they have assumed, for all of their existence, that they are their mind, rather than that they possess a mind.

The two concepts are quite different, and while one positions you as a victim, ending as another patient depending on antidepressants, the other concept leads you towards the strategies that are necessary to overcome any problem.

What I said about running was just one example. If you can't run or don't feel like running, you can simply go for long walks.

During one of my breakups, I literally spent months just walking, while listening to motivational podcasts.

When I got tired of walking around the same city, I decided to travel to seven countries, and go to music festivals by myself.

I felt great! And eventually, found my way into a new reality, by moving to a new country.

The decision was easy to make, as I always go where my heart flows.

If I make many friends in a city, that's the city where I go. I don't think much about it.

I learned to act like this, because I realized that, quite often, the best way to solve a problem, is to remove yourself from the equation, and all the things in that equation that bring forth more memories.

Some times, changing house is enough to accomplish this goal.

As for what regards physical activity, anything has a positive outcome.

Other activities I practiced during the most difficult periods of my life, were climbing mountains, kayaking, and playing archery.

You can choose anything you want. It doesn't have to be only from the examples I named.

One of my friends, a professional programmer, once I explained this to him, decided to subscribe to salsa dancing classes. And interestingly, that's where he ended up finding the love of his life.

HOW TO GET LUCKY: HOW TO CHANGE YOUR MIND AND GET ANYTHING IN LIFE

Another thing to take into consideration here, are your own emotions, as you shouldn't do things that make you feel like you are putting more efforts, but rather participate in sports or other activities in which you are enjoying yourself. Because you do want to change your emotions as well.

Chapter 24 — How to Control Your Emotions.

A great way to change our emotions is comedy.

In this highly depressive and suppressive world, that's not easy! But you can always find movies and podcasts that are dedicated only to comedy.

I used to spend hours just listening to the comedians in those shows. And during the worse moments of my life, that helped me change the way I see myself and my experiences.

Comedy is a great way to help us overcome our moments of depression.

That doesn't mean we should ignore our negative thoughts or negative emotions, contrary to popular belief. It simply means you don't let them control you.

There should be moments also to cry, to let the memories come to the surface, and to process them. But you shouldn't do that at home. You should do that as you walk, or in some place where nobody can see you, but outside. Because it makes the whole situation easier to overcome.

The more you connect to your emotions, the less they control you.

As an exercise, focus on these steps:

- **Step One** — Which emotions do you feel? Let's choose one!

- **Step Two** — From one to ten, how much do you feel that emotion?

- **Step Three** — Focus on that feeling, and let it come out!

- **Step Four** — Now, how strong is that feeling, from one to ten?

- **Step Five** — Repeat this exercise until the feeling is gone.

- **Step Six** — Continue to do this exercise for all your suppressed memories, until you have none that is tormenting you.

Remember that it is ok to feel anger, disgust, hatred, resentment, and sadness. But you shouldn't live your entire life with those feelings. You must process them.

One of the gravest mistakes of many therapists, is that they induce their patients to suppress their emotions, or ignore them. You should never do that!

The purpose of your emotions is to help you understand yourself and your reality. You need them to survive, to be who you are, and to gain a higher sense of sanity.

Your emotions protect you. And you need to learn to process the negative emotions, if you wish to be stronger with the emotions you need to live with — courage, ambition, happiness, and trust.

After many disappointments in my life, I can tell you that I don't waste any more time thinking about anyone. If a relationship fails, and fails for reasons that I won't ever forgive, such as continuous lies, manipulations, and someone raising her voice on me, I ask that person to pack her things and leave.

After that, I go back to my work, as if nothing had happened.

Sure, I feel disappointed and sad, and I may need weeks, even months, to overcome the separation. But I won't stop because of it. In fact, I quickly turn to activities that change my vibration and emotions, by watching comedies, and doing more sports outside.

Some people may try to shame you for acting strong, as they often do to me. And in regard to those situations, let me tell you this: I have been called cold and unloving, without feelings. But many of the women who used these words, cheated on me over time. So what I learned is that, people shame you to get what they want. The insults are just more tactics of manipulation.

HOW TO GET LUCKY: HOW TO CHANGE YOUR MIND AND GET ANYTHING IN LIFE

Today, I know that loving myself is more important than loving someone else. So when someone says I don't love, I reply that I do, 'I do love myself enough not to tolerate disrespect from anyone'.

Yes, it is sad, when you trust someone who betrays you, or when you have to break up with someone, just because she decided to shout in the house. But even sadder is to waste years of your life with such individuals. Because they are not likely to change.

People can change, they just won't if they don't have to.

Quite often, takes them years of disappointments, of failed marriage after failed marriage, for them to learn their lessons. However, many never do. They put the blame somewhere else, to protect their self-image and neglect the need to do all that work on themselves.

Chapter 25 — Never Count on Support During Hard Times.

Another important thing you must remember, is to never ever reveal to anyone, including your spouse, the goals you have in life. Because most people have negative assumptions.

Most people assume, by default, that others always fail to change themselves or their results.

I have never met one single person that truly believes in that possibility.

A lot of people say they do, they claim to be positive, and then you look at what they do, and it becomes obvious how negative they are.

Whenever I face problems in life, all those positive thinkers and religious do-gooders disappear from sight.

They are selfish, negative, and frightened creatures, that don't believe a person running on bad luck can ever change his situation.

These are the same people who want to spend time with me when they feel I am running on good luck. They think this luck can be taken by association.

That's why I call them selfish. They are disgusting.

Every single time I was on very bad luck, I was able to change my situation. But not even once, have I met one person, that believed I would.

What ends up happening, is that people get surprised when I am able to change my situation, and make more money after losing it, or find a more beautiful girlfriend than the previous one.

They say, 'Oh, you are so lucky'. And in my mind I can only think, 'And you are so damn stupid.'

Quite a lot of these people only show up in my life during my highs. They vanish during my lows. And that's why I have removed more than a thousand people from my life.

Again, they will call you selfish, cruel, etc. But the point is, you don't want to be surrounded by such parasites. And that's what most people are — parasites.

They want to take from you, whatever it is — your joy, your luck, your attitude. Because they can't produce it themselves, they won't pay for a book, they won't read anything.

That's all they can do. That's their nature!

In some cases, I waited for more than twenty years, to see if such people would change. They didn't!

There are certain characteristics in people that just don't change. They either have it or they don't.

Chapter 26 — Why People Lose Their Luck and How to Get it Back.

Luck is not always permanent. You can lose it.

You can lose your luck for many reasons, among which the most relevant is being associated with the wrong personalities. And unfortunately, most people think that in order to make themselves lucky, they have to make you miserable.

In all the relationships in which the person I was with saw life in that way, she tried to make me lose money, by trying to persuade me to do things that would lead me astray from my goals.

That is particularly common if you meet narcissists. Narcissists only sleep with the people they admire.

They copy such people, to get as much as they can, but at the same time, try to destroy them.

The ultimate goal of the narcissist, is to take as much as possible from the victim — often the spouse — and then leave the victim in complete misery. And they usually do that, under the disguise of love or a strong friendship.

They praise you until they can manipulate you.

The amount of narcissists in society keeps increasing, even though everyone is a narcissist to a greater or lesser extent.

So what do I mean by 'increasing'? I mean that people are becoming narcissistic beyond what should be accepted. They are at a dangerous level right now. And this dangerous level comes from the scarcity mindset I mentioned here.

Energies are contagious, and a person with a scarcity mindset will influence your own energy. That is why rich people don't like to be near the poor.

You are the people you surround yourself with, energetically, in thoughts, and in achievements.

You should not want to be near people who will not only remain in a lower position, but also drag you down.

There is no nice way to say this: If you spend time with people that have a scarcity mentality, a selfish view on life, a competitive mindset, in which they think they must take from others what they don't have, their energy will make you less able as a person.

If you want to evaluate the people you know, to see how safe you are near them, think in terms of jealousy and trauma.

How jealous are they when you get something they wish to have?

Do you see them biting the lip in anger, or frustrated because they can't get the same?

Sometimes, among women, that's just about having a better man.

Women hate when their friend finds a type of man they can't find for themselves.

In terms of trauma, this means talking about a situation that hurts you. See how your friends respond!

For example, if I talk about a breakup with male friends, they all vanish. Very few will stay. Among those who stay, many will use the situation to humiliate me.

That's how I know their nature.

This strategy makes it easier to know the kind of people that surround you. The bad news is that you'll realize that the vast majority is trash.

Among one thousand friends I made in the past four years, I only talk to five of them now.

Chapter 27 — How to Change Your Personal Vibration.

The challenge in getting what you want, is usually related to your vibrational nature.

That, as mentioned before, is affected by the people that know you, and how they perceive you — their own visualizations, their memories of you, and how they see you —, but also by yourself, and how you see yourself.

You can't pretend to be someone you are not. So how can you be the person you want to become?

The trick here is to let your visualizations change you.

When you close your eyes, and you think about that boat or house, or car you want to have, consider how it would make you feel and change.

Do you like such changes in you?

Probably, with more money, you will feel more confident, you will feel less worried about your present situation — which will then be your past —, and you will also feel more able than other people you know.

The more you think about all those possibilities, all the changes that will transform your spirit and your own nature as a person, the more you will, by association, change.

That exercise will make you prepared for the transformations coming your way. Because you will no longer think about the opportunities as an old you, but rather a future you, a new you.

You will, more clearly, understand what you must do as well.

As you do the things you now see that you must do, the more you will change. And step by step, you get closer to your goal.

Nevertheless, you must be willing to change yourself, and become a new type of person, with new ideas, new perspectives, and so on.

For example, if you think rich people are evil — and usually poor people think so —, do you really think you want to make more money? You don't! Because then you will see yourself as a bad person, and you don't want to be bad, you want to be admired as a good person.

So instead, you must consider what type of good person is rich. See the difference?

Once I started doing this exercise with myself, it became easier to distinguish the greedy rich from the altruistic rich. And sure, most rich people are evil, because most of the society is evil.

Most of the poor and most of the middle-class people are evil too.

In fact, you are more likely to find evil in the poor class than the rich, because the poor class is fighting for survival.

Most criminals will tell you that they don't know how to do anythings but steal. They never studied, never went to college, and never learned anything else.

A rich person, has at least that choice. And having a choice makes all the difference.

Chapter 28 — Money Does Not Make People Evil.

You can choose whatever you want to do with your money.

Without money, you have no choice. You can be a very good person without money, but you can't do much for the world.

If you have money, you can save the animals, protect the forests, and feed the poor.

Do you think I could help you if I had no time to write books?

The reason why I can write books is because I make more money now than I did before.

When people ask me for free books, not only are they insulting my existence, but acting against theirs too.

It comes from that scarcity and selfish mentality, that one must get everything at no cost, for free if possible.

Such people forget that starving authors can't write books.

How many homeless people do you see typing a book in a MacBook? None!

If you want your favorite authors to write, pay for their work — buy all the editions of every book you want, contact them to pay them more, make sure they know how much you appreciate them.

Don't pay more to the priest in the church in charity than you pay an author. That's foolish! It's an insult to God.

If there were no books, there would be no Bible, Quran, Vedas, Upanishads, etc.

Books are prior to religions. Without books, there would be no religions.

Respect the authors of the knowledge you receive, as you respect God for the miracles coming to your life!

Never, ever, assume that you are taking from God, or using God, or that if God favors you, it is because he doesn't like other people.

That foolish mistake can make you lose everything you get.

Respect the need of others to make money, if you want to attract more to your life!

Chapter 29 — How to Uplift Your Emotions.

The more energy you put in your visualizations, the more likely you are to attract what you want. But how do you raise your energy level?

You do that with love. You must be passionate about the things you want to get.

Those things must excite you. Thinking about having them, must bring joy to you.

Your emotions will raise your energy levels.

These emotions can be activated with smells. You know, the smell of an old house is very different from the smell of a new house.

The same applies to old cars and new cars.

You know there is something about what uplifts you that pulls your attention to it and makes you feel excited about it.

The same I could say about music. Music has emotion. When you day-dream with music, it's easier.

Another thing you can do, is visit rich houses for sale, like the one you want to have, or pretend to go buy a car like the one of your dreams.

The more you do this, the more you put yourself in the vibration of having it, because you are changing yourself in the process.

The way you dress also affects how you feel about yourself. It is difficult to feel rich when you are dressing in a poor way.

You should have, at least, one suit or dress that makes you feel empowered, confident and wealthy.

Everything that you can consider to uplift your mood and make you feel good, will work to help you increase your energy levels.

You must think and feel like a lucky person, before you can actually attract luck.

Now, what happens if you get unlucky sometimes? You don't talk about it, you ignore that situation, and you keep on trying to be lucky again.

Lucky people, all have moments of lack of luck.

Those who call me lucky, have no idea of how many times I have been unlucky.

People see you as lucky because they focus on your wins, not losses. So there's really no point in feeding their negative assumptions about you, or yours, by thinking about losses. Just keep moving forward, and ignore the moments in which you don't win whatsoever it is.

When I end a relationship, I don't think, 'Oh, I am so unlucky with women'.

I think, 'I wonder what type of person I will find next!', and surely enough, I always meet more and more interesting and beautiful women, beyond my expectations.

The same applies to money.

I never think, 'Oh, I am losing money this month', but rather, 'I wonder how can I make more next month'.

By changing my viewpoint, and putting the responsibility over the results on me, rather than outside of me, I am able to change my vibration towards attracting more luck.

That is how I am able to change my situations.

Chapter 30 — How to Master Success and Luck.

Nobody talks about the many failures that all the successful entrepreneurs had in the past. They talk about their successes. And what about authors? Do you know how many never sold one single copy?

I have met some of those authors, that never sold anything. As with other people, they also think I am lucky.

That's why they are so unlucky. They think I have a secret they must steal.

It's pathetic too, to notice that.

In truth, the reason why some authors seem to be lucky, while others, the majority of them, aren't, is that authors who are lucky, don't waste time with their lack of luck. They don't overwhelm themselves with their first book.

They just love to write and keep writing. And they write more, and more, and more, until someone finally notices them.

Perfection is the mother of mastery, and mastery of an art is what produces the luck of the artist.

It is easy to be lucky if you work hard enough for it. The harder you work, the luckier you will seem to everyone else.

Another reason why people call me lucky, comes from my sales. They think I woke up one day and decided to sell bestsellers. And that having more than one hundred bestsellers is the result of luck.

Indeed, I can say that getting those books into the best selling charts within weeks, was luck. But the person who wrote them did not become lucky spontaneously. My background experience is far superior to any one of my age, and superior to what anyone would believe.

I have taught in public universities and primary schools. I have managed many companies as human resources manager. And I have also worked for many religious organizations during my entire life. And I did all of that while working as a business consultant and creating several businesses of my own.

My background is not necessarily related to writing, but I consume a huge abundance of knowledge for many years. I can even listen to interviews as I sleep and write while listening to podcasts.

That puts me in a very different level, considering only accumulated knowledge. Much more I could say, in terms of work I did with myself and my mind, the amount of hours of meditation I practice since I am twelve years old, and a lot more.

Believe me, my luck is the result of a long process. And yet, as mentioned before, everyone is gifted with the same opportunities. They merely have to act on them.

As a matter of fact, the less you worry about your failures, in the future or from the past, the more likely you are to win. Because worry has a vibration as well.

When you worry about something, that's your mind telling you that it hasn't overcome that vibration of failure. But the more you succeed, the less important failure is to you.

The people who are more scared of failing, are those who never won. If you win more, you simply win more, because you aren't worried about possible negative outcomes.

If Picasso was still alive, his new paintings would be worth a fortune. But what about the first paintings? Do you think his first paintings were worth much, when nobody knew who he was?

Picasso was once at a Paris market when an admirer approached and asked if he could do a quick sketch on a paper napkin for her.

Picasso politely agreed, promptly created a drawing, and handed back the napkin — but not before asking for a million Francs.

HOW TO GET LUCKY: HOW TO CHANGE YOUR MIND AND GET ANYTHING IN LIFE

The lady was shocked: 'How can you ask for so much, if it took you only five minutes to draw this!', she said.

Picasso replied, 'No, it took me 40 years to draw this in five minutes'.

Chapter 31 — Why Most Artists and Authors Have No Luck.

It is easier to change your vibration, if you also learn to look at life as a game.

In order to do this, I will teach you a simple game you can play every day.

Choose a small container, anything you like, or just a plastic bag, and put inside more than thirty pieces of paper, each one with something you are thankful for.

Every day, you must do two things: one is take any paper by chance, to see what you should be thankful for that day. And another is to add one more paper for what you are thankful that day.

Soon, you will find that you have a lot of things to be thankful for.

The daily practice will make you look at life from another angle, and keep your vibration at the highest level — hope, expectation, deserving and faith.

The longer you keep yourself in this frequency, the more likely you are to attract more things that will make you feel appreciated and grateful.

Quite often, the problem with most people, is that they consistently maintain an aura of being outside the luck spectrum. Such thing is an impossibility by default, unless they wish to maintain themselves there, permanently.

We all heard stories of painters and writers who died poor and only after years passed was their work recognized and valued.

They would be extremely rich if they were alive today. But why did that happen?

For the vast majority, those artists and writers were without luck. And so, most people think that only what is old has value, and they don't read the works of the writers who are alive, they don't value the paintings of artists who are alive today as much as they value the works of dead ones.

Those attitudes towards art and books reflect the mindset of the majority.

However, if we travel back in time, and look carefully at the lives of those artists and writers, we see that they never truly tried to overcome their barriers and manifest their dreams.

In other words, they were too busy with their art and writing, and not really investing in advertising themselves.

In many other cases, they had poor marketing skills, and their work never went very far.

In other words, they had no interest in sharing their work. They were interested only in producing it.

The same happens with many artists and writers of today's world. They expect other people to recognize their talent.

They are waiting for luck to manifest in their lives, while at the same time, most people don't even know they exist.

The interesting thing about professional gamblers, is that they hold a very different mindset. They think like a seller. They know that they can't lose all the time.

You see, a professional seller doesn't quit with the first 'no'. He keeps trying, again and again, and improving his methods to advertise a product, until eventually he makes the sales he needs. And the same applies to the gambler. He tries many times until he finds himself running on luck.

In both cases, they know that it's not possible to lose all the time.

The same principle applies to dating, which is, quite frankly, a numbers game.

Professional pick-up artists, simply know that if they approach enough women, some will eventually reply positively. They are just not wondering about it or avoiding rejection.

They are expecting rejection as a likely event. They just don't focus on it.

HOW TO GET LUCKY: HOW TO CHANGE YOUR MIND AND GET ANYTHING IN LIFE

Now, going back to the frustrated artists and authors, if they actually believed in their work, and tried different methods of advertising, eventually, they would come across someone that would buy their paintings and books, and their fame would then come sooner.

When we are trying to get lucky, we must remind ourselves, like anyone else who gets lucky in life, that there are many moments of bad luck as well. We simply take them for granted.

We must look at bad luck as just a moment in life.

The difference requires discernment. We must be able to know when to try our luck and when to wait for it.

In time, this ability is developed, and the more experience we have in attracting luck, the more our sixth-sense, our ability to make decisions in the right time, and to make the right decisions, will help us.

Chapter 32 — How to Avoid Failure.

I was once asked, during a public speaking on the topic of success, how do we avoid failure.

My answer was simple but not properly understood.

I said: 'You don't avoid failure. You simply fail.'

The question that followed then was: 'So how do you know when you are going to succeed in what you do?'

The answer is simple too: With experience, comes discernment. And even though you don't always know everything, you do know when the odds are in your favor or against you.

A reader once asked me: 'If you know so much about the law of attraction, why don't you use it to win the lottery?'

The reason why is related to what I explained above. I don't like to play games where I am more likely to lose.

I don't talk to women who don't smile at me, I don't try to convince people who don't want to read my books, I don't spend time explaining myself to people who disrespect me, and I don't play lottery games, because there are just too many people playing them.

The reason why I am lucky, is because I make myself the most favorable element in the game I choose to play.

In other words, it seems I am lucky with women, because I only approach those who seem interested in talking to me. I seem lucky with books, because I only write about things I know well. And I am loved by many people, because I am not trying to persuade selfish people to appreciate what I do.

Now, when you combine all that energy, it is easy to predict luck. It comes in the form of more opportunities and ideas.

The opposite is also true. That is, when I am losing money, I start searching for reasons. When I find them, I change the situation.

I never spend my time, for example, with people who have no trust in my capacity to attract money. That's bad energy!

As you see, just as with professional gamblers, it is all about increasing your odds of winning. And in time, you develop that inner sense that tells you when you are more likely to win.

This spiritual sense will be perfected for any situation. When I was a child, my family members always asked me to help them play luck games, because the numbers I chose were always right, at least, some of them.

Later in life, my friends also realized this talent in me. So they started inviting me to go to casinos with them. Once we even had the security guards asking us to leave, because we were winning too much.

However, I was operating on instinct. That was the reason why my decisions seemed to attract luck. I didn't always win.

I remember once that one of my friends decided to go crazy, and invest a lot of money on the numbers I told him to choose. But, if he had won until then, in that last attempt, he lost all the money.

He was frustrated with me, but anyone that works in gambling houses and casinos knows that the machines are rigged to make the person fail once in a while. So even with my best intentions, I couldn't fight that machine.

I did advise my friend not to gamble anymore, but he got greedy.

Knowing how to win, also demands knowing when not to play to win.

Chapter 33 — Luck as a Science.

Scientific studies on the topic of luck, such as the one conducted by Dr. Richard J. Wiseman — Professor of the Public Understanding of Psychology at the University of Hertfordshire in the United Kingdom —, concluded that lucky people do create their own luck, by being in a different mindset when compared to the unlucky people.

Unlucky people are afraid to take advantage of the opportunities in front of them, while lucky people create their own opportunities.

That means changing routines often, talking to strangers, changing the conversation style, trying different types of food, or simply avoiding saying certain words we tend to use in a daily basis.

Those changes make us more flexible, and mentally more adaptable to change, which in turn, will make us more connected to our sense of purpose in life and the streams of luck in our way.

These constant changes also make us less afraid to catch new opportunities when they are right in front of us.

Another thing that was found is that lucky people are more likely to adapt to an uncertain future, while unlucky people stick more to plans.

Even though this doesn't mean that planning for the future is a bad idea, the interesting thing about unlucky people is that they maintain their plans, even when reality shows them that the plan is failing, i.e., they are unable to change their decisions.

On the other hand, although lucky people don't plan as much, they are very well-connected, and maintain a large group of friends around them. This makes it easy for them to find new opportunities, whenever their life is not going in the direction they want.

Unlucky people tend to be isolated, so they don't have access to so many opportunities as lucky people do.

However, the type of friends that lucky people make are not random. It was found in the researches that lucky people tend to be better observers, and try to make friends with people that create a win-win situation, i.e., individuals that have a higher sense of abundance, are more likely to start a conversation and are more empathetic.

They are team players, so they are more likely to talk to people who have this type of mentality.

Due to this predisposition for change, lucky people tend to create patterns of understanding that makes them better at detecting opportunities as well.

In the book, 'Chance and Luck' by Richard A. Proctor, there are examples of many famous personalities in history and how they perceived their own luck.

Napoleon would announce that a certain star seen in full daylight was his star — and indicated at the moment the ascendency of his fortune —, and William the Conqueror proclaimed, as he rose with hands full of earth from his accidental fall on the Sussex shore, that he was destined by fate to seize England.

Even though one may argue that Napoleon imagined star was the planet Venus, bound to be where Napoleon and his officers saw it, by laws which it had followed for past millions of years, and will doubtless follow for millions of years to come, or that William fell because of certain natural conditions affecting him physiologically (as probably he was excited and over anxious) and physically, and not by any influence affecting him extra-naturally, the fact is that such situations play on the mind of a winner like the gambler's superstitions.

Chapter 34 — The Signs of Luck in the Environment.

Conditions that can be calculated and studied from a scientific perspective, are for the gamblers and the winners in battle, merely patterns that show them success on the way.

If we take into consideration that Napoleon was a freemason, and member of a family of famous freemasons of his time, it is only natural that he would apply laws of visualization, that would then manifest in his life, to help him identify the right moments for war.

The same we can say about William the Conqueror, for he was a Knight Templar.

These are men who truly believe God is on their side, and therefore learn to interpret the signs that represent their visions and dreams when manifested in reality.

What for others is subject of personal belief, for these men is a true spiritual science.

Lucky people can then be seen as spiritual and bound to faith, even though their faith is guided by patterns, symbols and signs.

The difference between this and the faith of the unlucky people, is that the unlucky ones have what we can call apathetic faith, meaning that they ignore the signs, they ignore the opportunities, potential paths, and adventures that manifest in their life.

They rather live a life of safety and security.

God answers both but the unlucky can't see it. And quite often, they don't see it because God acts through other people. And as the unlucky people are looking for paths coming from God Himself, direct paths, they ignore these other people.

I noticed that religious people, for example, never trust the words of anyone outside their congregation, and in particular, of those who studied different religions. And that is what makes them unlucky.

They can then say, 'Oh, but God loves the poor and hates the rich', and that's a lie that they perpetuate and tell themselves to satisfy their own laziness and comfort within the group.

They rather share misery than be broken apart by luck. Because, for sure, once you get lucky in a group of unlucky people, you will be looked upon with disdain and jealousy.

In fact, that's how all friendships break apart between me and the members of these groups. They see me as gifted and them as ungifted. But because they consider themselves holy and special — in a childlike mentality and view of themselves —, they must consider me their opposite, and influenced by demonic forces.

In their mental justifications, they then finds reasons to provoke me, insult and depart, so they can maintain their self-image of perfection.

This is exactly what narcissists do. Religious people have a strong inclination to narcissism. And that's exactly what makes them evil.

If you ever wondered why most religious people are evil, you just got your answer.

Religion doesn't make people evil. Dogma and arrogance does. That's how narcissism manifests. And narcissism is the gateway to hell. For narcissists are either demonically influenced or spiritually possessed.

Chapter 35 — How Expectations Can Determine Results.

The methodology of visualization is more effective when we visualize the process rather than the end point.

When kings and emperors visualized their victories, they didn't just see the goal they wanted to achieve, but also the entire process to achieve it. That's what made them recognize the patterns of success when such were present.

In this sense, if one wishes to be lucky, he should visualize himself as a lucky person, and not just having money. That process is much more powerful for the mind.

As an example, if you want to be rich, you don't just visualize yourself with money, but also talking, acting and behaving, like people who have money.

That would be comparable to acting, but it's exactly what children do, when they imitate adults or their favorite actors in movies. They are learning by imitation, and in doing so, changing their neurological patterns accordingly.

It is said that children born in poor families are more likely to fail in school and in life, not necessarily because they were born poor, but because they were not given the right conditions.

Many scientific studies in the field of education, show us that the patterns of communication that parents have at home, have a strong influence on the capacity of a child to understand the more elaborated and complex forms of communication in their books and coming from their teachers.

It is then with no surprise that the children of business owners, doctors, nurses and other professions viewed as more elitist by society, do better in school, than the children of cleaning maids and construction workers.

One of the most offensive things teachers still do to this day, and all over the world, is to question children about the profession of their parents in the first day of school, because if sets the precedent that intelligence is permanent and attributed to genes. It then allows discriminating those children accordingly.

Such teachers, as studies indicate, tend to behave with the children accordingly, by leveling their expectations according to the professions of the parents.

What studies also show us, is that when teachers believe that their students are smart, they then tend to act accordingly, by having higher expectations and giving them more attention in the classroom. As a result, the students do improve their grades significantly.

Chapter 36 — Can We Relearn How to Think?

In my experience as an expert in learning disabilities, one of the things that was always obvious to me, is that teachers and parents keep insisting on the premise that if a child is not doing well, he or she needs more work. If the child refuses to work or complains, he or she is labeled as lazy.

Then, if that still doesn't produce results, rather than blaming their methods, they blame the child again. And this time, they will take the child to a psychologist, that will then label him with some mental disorder, and act towards the child in this manner, by using teaching methods that do nothing more than change the conditions of the child.

As I noticed by talking to all of these psychologists, there is no difference between the exercises they do and the ones produced by the teachers.

If anything, their exercises tend to condition the child to a certain thinking path as if the child was mentally retarded, because that's exactly how they see the child.

The methods I was using, to rehabilitate these children and make them go, not from abnormal to normal, but rather from abnormal to geniuses — with the best grades in the whole school, and within months — had nothing to do with having more work, or aids to study that will make them analyze information like some moron.

Instead, those methods intended to teach the child to think.

The reason why nobody could help them, is because nobody was ever thought how to think. The general population goes through life attributing their results to their birth conditions and luck.

Many of the questions I would ask a child, consisted of 'Show me why you think you are right'.

I never accepted that, 'One and one equals two because the teacher says so", but rather asked them to show me that one object plus one object equals two objects by actually making them look at those objects.

We would then do similar exercises in math and history with play-doh, lego, stones, and other objects we could use, either inside or outside the classroom.

It was by making them see and understand how to think better, that their grades improved.

These children, quite expectably, became rebels against the system, for they used to say: 'Why do I need to work so hard, if I can just play and get better grades?'

You see, they understood that you become better by visualizing patterns in the real world. And that is a more important lesson than education can give them.

Education can give them knowledge. But I gave them the power to be anyone they want to be and attract all the luck they wish to have. By teaching these children on how to observe patterns and to think over the information received, I gave them the ability to analyze reality itself. This is the source of luck.

As I observed, these children didn't just became the best students of the whole school overnight. They also changed their personality from one extreme to another. They became more confident, happier, and more communicative.

They also went from being isolated, apathetic or aggressive, to actually organizing games with other children.

That's the route from introversion to extroversion, that separates the unlucky from the lucky ones.

One can then say, "Yes, but many geniuses are introverted", about which I can agree.

The problem is that many geniuses also die miserably and unknown because they are unlucky, and they are unlucky precisely because they are introverted.

HOW TO GET LUCKY: HOW TO CHANGE YOUR MIND AND GET ANYTHING IN LIFE

Even though there is no correlation between being a genius and being introverted, as we see in many examples, such as with the cases of Pablo Picasso or Ernest Hemingway, there is certainly a correlation between being introverted and unlucky, as with the cases of Nikola Tesla and Vincent van Gogh.

Chapter 37 — How Do We Create 'Better Thoughts'?

Gay Hendricks, in his book 'Conscious Luck', maintains the idea that lucky people are indeed determined by their own thoughts.

In the book, he explains this state as being in harmony with the events that happen to us, even when they seem to bring us bad luck.

Lucky people never fail to see opportunities, even when for many of us, the situation seems unlucky.

Richard Wiseman, uses as an example a woman that thought of herself as lucky, despite the fact that, in the span of a month, her house had burnt down, her dog had run away, and, on the way to the fire department, she got into a car accident and broke her leg.

She said it was the best thing that ever happened to her because, when she was at the hospital, there was this cute nurse who was attending to her, and they got married.

If it was not for that tragedy in her life, they wouldn't have met.

In her view, it was the best month of her life.

She felt lucky because of all those events that led her to what was seen as a long-term happiness.

Lucky people can see how certain negative events bring them exactly to where they should be, situations which they wouldn't deliberately choose by themselves, unless those bad events had occurred to them. And so, they understand, as Gay Hendricks explains, that luck is like a wind we have to catch like a bird.

It's a flow of energy that harmonizes the good and the bad.

This is certainly true because one of my dreams was to visit Malaysia and Indonesia, and I would never go there if it wasn't for a relationship I had with a business owner that had clients in those countries.

Our relationship wasn't good, and eventually ended, but if I had not met her, I would probably not visit those countries. She asked me to go with her, because she was afraid to go alone.

She also asked me to help her in the meetings with the clients, which eventually helped me understand how rich people think, helping me make better decisions for my own business.

She never helped me. That's why the relationship ended.

She was a very selfish and self-centered narcissist. But by helping her, I ended up helping myself.

I didn't really know that those events would lead me to where I am today, but they certainly did. So I can't really be regretful for the bad experiences.

The same I could say about the people who got me fired from my jobs with gossip and false rumors. Those malevolent personalities, pushed me to move forward in life.

If it wasn't for them, I would never try to become a full-time writer and travel the world as one.

As anyone else, I was trying to find a safe job for life.

Those evil personalities, with their bad intentions, actually helped me fulfill my dream of being a full-time author.

If they were not in my life, I would certainly not push myself so hard, and write more than three hundred books to make my dream manifest itself.

This was particularly true when I found myself alone in Spain, after my relationship with that Chinese business owner was over, because now I had to definitely find a way to pay my rent with books only.

HOW TO GET LUCKY: HOW TO CHANGE YOUR MIND AND GET ANYTHING IN LIFE

I went to the beach about three times, despite living in front of it. I spent those two years in Spain working like mad, from 5AM to midnight, every single day, from Monday to Sunday.

Chapter 38 — How Lucky People Overcome Difficulties.

Lucky people don't succumb to their fate, and then rethink over their lack of fortune. Instead, they find gaps, signs, and even reasons within their situation, that tell them they are heading towards good luck.

That requires intuition but also discernment and patience.

The lucky ones, seek for the advantages when life changes for them. They seek for new paths when the previous ones close. And that's how they find themselves in lucky situations, as with the case of the woman who found her husband after all the traumatic events in her life that pushed her towards finding him.

Again, I can identify myself with this situation. For as I grow older, the women that enter my life keep getting younger and more beautiful. And the reason why, is that I don't try to find them. Instead, I am merely observing more the signs around me.

While most men have a scarcity mentality and chase after women, I simply talk to the women that appear in my life without any second intention. Then, as the conversation goes, I start to understand where it may lead.

That's why one of my girlfriends was a hairdresser, after I got rejected by more than ten different ones, when trying to find a place to cut my hair, and others were graphic designers, due to my need to change the design of my book covers that led me to find them and talk to them.

I don't just attract women that are somehow related to what I need to do, but also women that are trying to find men like me. The lucky opportunity appears simply because I perceive it in the environment.

We can call that instinct or being extroverted, but in truth, I don't just talk to anyone I encounter, and I rarely start conversations with strangers.

I will talk to a woman if there is something about her that is related to me. Those are the signs I observe (as Napoleon also did).

If a woman has a necklace with a pentagram, or some other form within sacred geometry, that is a reason for me to start a conversation.

Tarot cards and tattoos about mythology is another reason that strikes my curiosity.

Interestingly, women that are into art and mysticism, do exactly that. And that's what makes the conversation and the chemistry predictable.

In fact, I noticed that these relationships only fail because of the lack of faith that these women have.

Many of them engage too much in their thoughts, and start doubting the obvious. It happens due to the plan we have in our head, that never changes despite the circumstances.

For example, many of these women decide to destroy the relationship because I travel a lot, and they are afraid I may abandon them. Or because I am a writer and they think writers are poor. They assume things instead of observing. And that's the cause of their lack of luck.

All of them think of themselves as being unlucky.

Many of these women are driven by their memories and fears, rather than their faith in the future.

That is another characteristic that differentiates the ones who have no luck from those who have it.

People that have no luck live in the past, or the present — which is the same as living the past, because if you are in the present, you are trying to escape the past.

People who claim to live in the present, are constantly comparing the present with the past. They literally talk about the past as if it was in the present.

HOW TO GET LUCKY: HOW TO CHANGE YOUR MIND AND GET ANYTHING IN LIFE

That's why all the philosophies of 'You must be in the here and now' are deceiving. For we didn't evolve by behaving like that, but by learning from the past to reprogram our hopeful views projected into the future.

We project better futures when we can learn from the mistakes of the past. And so, lucky people attract luck because they live in the future. They live in that present-future, and they are constantly looking for opportunities to manifest it. And that, well, demands a certain dose of risk.

You minimize the risk when you see the signs. That's observation over memory or fear.

Every opportunity brings forth fear and risk.

There is no such thing as perfect manifestation. But because people seek for that perfection, as the Disney movies from their childhood and other Hollywood movies they watch as adults persuade them to be true, they constantly seek for that movie scrip that has no correlation to reality. In doing that, they miss all the great opportunities in their life.

Chapter 39 — Loneliness as a Strategy in Change.

One of the saddest things about the society we have today, is that people are extremely conditioned to be competitive.

When you are facing a bad moment in life, people take that as an opportunity to step on you, or hypocritically position themselves above you, either with advice that does nothing good for you, or by criticizing your actions and decisions.

The problem with that, is that it delays and even shifts your vibration away from your goals — as well as your attention —, and from finding the opportunities ahead.

Those people victimize you and make you a target for more lack of luck.

When one of my relationships ended and I was losing money, most of my friends disappeared, and the few friends I had, many of them in different religious congregations, took the opportunity to step on me with their overrated sense of moral superiority.

They would indirectly insult me or make me feel inferior. And as a result, I had to cut all those people from my life.

It is difficult, when you are already in a wave of bad luck, to decide for total loneliness. But that's actually the only way out of the situation.

Eventually, by opening more space in my life, new people enter it. I got more time to write, more ideas, I traveled more as well, precisely because I was bored and with no social life, and eventually, I wrote better books, made more money, and met better women.

My life got better, I had more money, and I traveled more.

That's when I realized that it is better to seek for support in God than people.

Most people are worthless garbage. They themselves are immersed in a wave of negative narcissism, a false sense of superiority, and bad luck.

If you want to change your life, you must have the courage to separate yourself from such individuals. Because that will help you move away faster from the situations that bring you bad luck.

As I usually say, it is actually good to lose friends in a city, because then I have no reasons to stay there anymore. It makes it easier to change to another city or country.

I travel a lot because I have no reasons to stay anywhere. If I had, I would stay. But I am seeking for those reasons to stay.

I rather be lucky that miserable.

Safety and security and comfort are illusions when we are not reaching our goals. And what I found is that, I may not have that feeling of comfort most of the times, but at the same time, I am lucky, I am achieving all my goals, and traveling a lot more than anyone I ever met.

This luck comes from the sense that I lose nothing, even when losing. And so, I reject the idea of being a victim that others try to impose on me, because they themselves have a poor view on life, and don't really understand it.

The vast majority of people are a fruit of randomness. They have no idea how to create success or luck. They are afraid of change. That's precisely why they are unlucky.

Many of them, especially the christians, want to think of themselves as being lucky, because they don't want to think they were abandoned by God, but what you see them actually doing is attributing luck to very basic and random events, like being married to some ugly woman they met in the congregation, or having a son and food on the table.

Those are basic necessities, and not attributed to luck or God!

HOW TO GET LUCKY: HOW TO CHANGE YOUR MIND AND GET ANYTHING IN LIFE

Sure, if your basic necessities are met, you will be happy. But what truly puts you in a divine wave, a wave of luck, is far above that. It has everything to do with achieving your dreams. And your dreams change. So your life changes with your dreams. That's what is normal!

I am not saying you must divorce often, or have a bunch of kids, but rather that having a house, a car, food and a job, are basic needs. Not goals!

A goal has to be related to changing yourself and becoming a better person. And there is no limit for that. You can always improve, you can always make more money, make more friends, and become happier.

Chapter 40 — How to Analyze Our Negative Experiences.

People who overcome adversity can be considered lucky as well.

According to Dr. Jude Miller Burke, they are able to overcome poor self-confidence and then become very successful. They do this by learning to control their emotions and how they interpret such emotions.

The results of this research correlated with what Dr. Richard Wiseman found, enabling him to resume the four principles used by lucky people:

- **Principle One:** They maximize the number of opportunities in their life, by focusing in networking and being open to new experiences;

- **Principle Two:** They listen to 'lucky hunches', by being more intuitive and focusing in their gut feelings;

Principle Three: They expect good fortune, and consider themselves lucky. The expectations then become self-fulfilling prophecies, as they persist more in the face of failure than unlucky people.

- **Principle Four:** They turn bad luck into good, by imagining how bad situations could be worse, and by not dwelling in ill fortune.

Lucky people also take more responsibility for their life, which helps in moving past bad events faster.

That doesn't mean lucky people don't feel fear. According to Billionaire and businessman Grant Cardone, fear and success are related. You don't expand unless you face your fears. That, naturally, means seeing fear as an opportunity to expand.

In one of his interviews in 2019 (In 'The Science of Success'), he mentions the example of punching a UFC champion like Connor McGregor. He says, "At least you will find out, that if you hit Conner, he hits you back, he will break your nose", which could be what he describes as a "breakthrough moment", for it would generate a lot of free press, and attention on the brand of the person punched.

Any situation can be turned into an opportunity, even the ones that scare us the most. That is the meaning of being lucky — when you see lucky opportunities in anything, from the most obvious to the most dramatic situations, and especially, when you can create them at any given moment.

According to John Richard Boyd — United States Air Force fighter pilot and Pentagon consultant —, the key to victory is to be able to create situations wherein one can make appropriate decisions more quickly than one's opponent.

Her termed that process OODA — Observe, Orient, Decide, and Act.

However, he states in his principle, that our ability to succeed in chaotic moments, comes fundamentally from orientation. Orientation is prior to observation and will drive our attention according to the intention.

Orientation also demands a rethinking and reframing of our own beliefs — it implies confronting our cognitive biases, ego, and limited perception of reality.

If we do that, we get a more realistic perception of what is real, and get less conditioned by our own previous orientations, i.e., our memories and subconscious mind.

Boyd resumes this by saying, "Fight the enemy, not the terrain", meaning: don't get stuck in analyzing what should be or what you would like the situation to be.

Chapter 41 — How the Ego Makes People Unlucky.

Chess championship winner, Joshua Waitzkin, explains that, the reason why most people fail is because they are locked to the need to be correct. They spend their time, and dedicate their focus, or orientation, to finding justifications to their situations, rather than moving out of them.

In other words, people who assume they are correct, never look at themselves to correct themselves.

Jim Paul — author of 'What I Learned Losing a Million Dollars' —, describes this state of mind as an association between self-worth and vicissitudes or factors beyond our control.

He says that, if you make such ties, you "will be primarily concerned with protecting your ego, rather than trying to determine the appropriate course of action."

You must be aware of your orientation — your beliefs and thoughts —, if you wish to control your results. Because that's the only way you will ever get a clear vision of reality.

It was found that, in both businesses and war, the most common mistake made was a decentralization of power, leaving the decision-making to the lowest ranks of the structure.

The more centralized and clear the vision is, the more likely a war is to be won and a business is to succeed.

That centralization is made of values and certain rules that are beyond our thoughts but guide them.

It doesn't matter how many people listen to you or how many don't; it doesn't even matter how much they understand of what you speak; or if you speak from a podium, or with a crown in your head, or not. It matters only that you live by your own values, no matter the consequences, for you and others around you. For you pay tomorrow for the decisions of today. And it's better to pay for investments than sorrows.

Chapter 42 — The Influence of Our Self-Image in Creating The Future.

Our existence, and more importantly, how we see ourselves, is the best scale of how successful we are in life. Those who fail live in shame and hide behind social masks.

As long as we are reaching our goals, and those goals allow us to look back and contemplate a vast spectrum of accomplishments, what others see, will never amount to more than a laugh on our part, if we are humble enough to realize how comic the topic of success is, either they see anything or see nothing, or see the exact opposite of what we accomplished and wish they could see. And that's the simplest and most effective definition of success to follow.

All measurements of success based on a social comparison are probably a measurement of failure, for you can't be successful in any system that compares your soul. Comparing your life purpose with others is the best way to lack an identity.

The reason why people suffer from anxiety and stress, is because they are constantly worried of what will happen to them from the perspective of how society judges their situation. This is related to the ego.

According to John Assaraf (In an interview to 'The Science of Success'), "The reason why people have a strong ego and beliefs they refuse to change is related to a whole world of emotions in their subconscious mind, and controlling their conscious decisions".

This is another way to say that our past — education, family values, culture, etc —, shapes our identity and that identity forms our ego.

The ego then becomes a static because we identity our self with that ego.

According to John Assaraf, "We have emotions that are triggered in the subconscious, that triggers neurochemicals that cause the feelings, that people either like or don't like, that they then resonate with or they don't".

These emotions are often irrational, and related to our past. And so, if a goal we want to achieve excites us and releases dopamine, and we then share it with a co-worker or a friend or a partner, and they release these oxytocin neurochemicals — bonding and love chemicals —, everybody feels great. However, if there's a subconscious pattern, for example, or a subconscious fear of failure or of being disappointed, then we are afraid of being embarrassed or ashamed and ridiculed.

According to John Assaraf, in these situations, "The neurochemicals of fear will actually stop people from taking action, and so, when we talk about emotions, those emotions are just signals for what's going on in your brain and through your body".

Quite often, what is triggering this disempowering or destructive emotion in us, is related to negative memories of the past still affecting our self-worth and our confidence in our results.

This is why people become apathetic and lose interest in creating their own future. Reason why they then, based on their failures, consider themselves unlucky.

As L. Ron Hubbard said, "All tiredness is willingness gone bad. People who are willing don't get tired. It's only when something makes them unwilling that they become exhausted. I could have somebody enthusiastically opening doors, and then all of a sudden fix it so that doors wouldn't open, and all of a sudden they're tired. So you say, 'Well, they opened doors 222 times and that made them tired.' Oh no it didn't! They opened doors 222 times and that made them feel pretty good. But the time they didn't find themselves able to open, the door tired them out. Not only is he unwilling to open the door, but he's unable to do so; and he becomes exhausted."

Chapter 43 — Could Luck Be Based on Belief?

Success is a measurement that is embedded in our subconscious mind, telling us that we can or can't do something, based on previous experiences of either success or failure. It is the idea that we can't face that which caused us frustration and suffering in the past.

People become unsuccessful and unlucky, quite simply, because they don't expect anything different than what their subconscious mind is telling them, through the emotions they feel.

We could even say that unlucky people are stuck in a past-present time moment. They are under the control of their subconscious mind.

How do we know that? They spend the whole time thinking and worrying about what can happen if something goes wrong, and by expecting it to go wrong, they actually attract the exact outcome that they simultaneously fear and expect to happen.

They then say, "I am so unlucky", while in fact, they created the situation that made that happen.

I remember one of my former girlfriends once telling me after our breakup, "I have no luck with men", while the reason for the breakup is that she had insulted me multiple times, shouted at me, and lied about a various amount of issues that were very important to me.

All she had to do was tell the truth, be honest and not shout at my face, for the relationship to work.

Sounds simple, doesn't it? But people who are incapable of looking at themselves, and instead perceive themselves as being perfect and with no need to change, rather put the blame of an outcome outside themselves. And that's exactly what characterizes an unlucky person — someone who is unable or unwilling to create her own luck.

So yes, she was unlucky, but by her own decision.

It is known in the mental health industry, that an individual is insane to the degree that he can't be responsible for his own actions. And that's exactly what happens to unlucky people. They attract different forms of mental illness by not being able to take full responsibility for their behaviors.

In doing so, they are then absorbed by compulsive thinking patterns, that revolve around their fears and self-made expectations.

Chapter 44 — How Victimization Leads to Self-Sabotage.

The ability to control our emotions, being these prior to our decisions and actions, is fundamental if we wish to control the amount of luck we get in life.

It is the difference between being in control of our life or being a victim of it.

Whenever we see ourselves as victims of our results, we end up self-sabotaging. Reason why, such individuals keep repeating the same experiences, and then considering themselves unlucky for not being able to change the outcome.

Every choice we make, being determined by emotions, has already set our destiny from the beginning.

If we then refuse to take responsibility for the outcome, that destiny becomes a fate that is easily predictable.

I was able to predict the fate of many people I met, simply by analyzing their own mental patterns.

I remember when once one of my girlfriends called me on the phone, saying: 'You were right, me and my new boyfriend are always fighting. I wish I had not cheated on you. You were better than him. We didn't fight so much.'

The reason why I was right in that prediction, is that I knew that our fights were all coming from her head. But people who are unable to confront themselves and change, always seek to find a scapegoat. And it's easier to blame-shift and project our faults into another person, rather than doing such work with our personality.

Such individuals, after concentrating all their faults in another, then imagine that with a new companion, such problems will vanish. After all, they have already projected all the problems in a person that won't be part of their life anymore.

This can be compared to dumping everything into a trashcan. Because that's exactly what narcissists and self-absorbed neurotic people do, as well as those who consider themselves unlucky in their relationships.

What then happens is that the cause, hidden in their subconscious, goes with them to manifest in the new partner. And after they leave this, unto the next.

Eventually, these people give up, and say things like, 'All men are the same', or 'All women are the same'. They fail to see the common denominator in all these similarities — themselves.

They fail to see it because they think they are a good person. And that's where the problems is — the egotistic idea that one did nothing wrong, even when it is obvious that she or he did.

These people can't analyze themselves because the psychologist to whom they pay, often doesn't want to lose a client, and as a result, doesn't have the courage to tell them the truth.

Their mother or father, or grandmother and grandfather, are also unable to tell them the truth, if they can even see it. And their friends don't want to lose any friend by speaking what they see.

Furthermore, the person who has a self-image of perfection, will always distort the facts, to maintain this idea that the problem is in another person. They repeat this false reality so much, that they end up believing it.

Then, they have some kind of amnesia, in regard to previous conversations in which agreements were made towards not engaging in a specific behavior, or following certain rules in the relationship.

They simply ignore what was spoken between two parties, to maintain their inner narrative.

It is as if such people were living under a script, that they keep repeating over and over again, no matter who is the person in front of them.

HOW TO GET LUCKY: HOW TO CHANGE YOUR MIND AND GET ANYTHING IN LIFE

They end up transforming all of their partners into the same actor that they have envisioned in their mind for the role of the bad guy.

This is exactly what women do in their relationships, when assuming all men are bad. They eventually find a good man, shout at him, insult him, and provoke him, until he reaches the limit, and tells them to get out of the house.

Once he does that, they are satisfied for being right and will say: 'See, I knew it, all men are bad, I was right from the start.'

If one man is not bad, that means she was wrong. And she doesn't want to be wrong. Accepting that one man can be good, means that she failed in all of her previous relationships. And this is a strong blow on the ego.

The person, to protect the ego, and a false identity of perfection, then rather repeat the same behaviors, again and again, no matter the characteristics of the person in front of them.

They keep searching for 'good men' and transforming all 'good men' into 'bad men'.

That's how unlucky people create bad luck.

I could use the exact same example for anything else, namely, people who can't cook.

I have met many women who can't cook, but never met one who said: "I am learning how to cook" or "I want to learn how to cook".

In many cases, I taught them how to cook, but they never wanted to cook what I taught them to cook, because that meant being able to cook, and being able to learn from a man. And they can't lie to their ego. So they simply pretend those classes I gave them never happened, just as they pretend the conversations I had with them on their behavior never happened as well.

We could even say that people are afraid to be happy, because being happy means admitting that one was wrong before, and that is a direct attack on the ego.

Instead, people self-sabotage their life and say, "I'm unlucky", or "Others are luckier than me", because that's a great way to avoid responsibilities over one's own results in life.

Chapter 45 — How to Eliminate The Negative Power of the Subconscious Mind.

Here's a set of questions you should ask yourself, to unlock the negative memories in your subconscious mind and trapping your decisions:

- Who said that I would never be successful? Describe the whole situation and the words spoken!

- Who made me feel unworthy? Describe the whole situation and the words spoken!

- Which events in the past made me feel unlucky? Describe the whole situation and the words spoken!

- When was the last time I felt undeserving? Describe how you felt!

- When was the last time I felt unloved? Describe how you felt!

- When was the last time I felt unlucky? Describe how you felt!

- When was the last time I felt disappointed? Describe how you felt!

- When was the last time I felt frustrated? Describe how you felt!

Now, grab a pen and a notebook, and write everything you can remember related to these questions.

Do this exercise often, in order to clean your subconscious mind from the negative influences of the past. The more you do this, the clearer your subconscious will be, and the less power it will have over your thoughts.

It is important that our intentions are not affected by counter-emotions, because, as John Assaraf says, "When we have an emotion that is going against our natural propensity for safety first, the brakes go on in our brain. The motivational center is deactivated."

It is only by eliminating our fears from the subconscious mind, that we are able to increase the power of that motivational center, from where our imagination and inspiration emerge.

Children don't have the same fear of failure, because they don't have the same burden of false expectations based on previous traumas that many of us have. That's why Jesus said, "Unless you change and become like little children, you will never enter the kingdom of heaven" (Matthew 18:3).

This heaven that he was speaking about is not a transcendental kingdom seen only after death or subject to religious dogma. Instead, it is a heaven that we can access by our own thoughts.

He explains this in Luke 17:21, by saying: "The kingdom of God is within you".

This explanation becomes even clearer in the Gospel Of Thomas, when he says the following:

"If those who lead you say, 'See, the Kingdom is in the sky,' then the birds of the sky will precede you. If they say to you, 'It is in the sea,' then the fish will precede you. Rather, the Kingdom is inside of you, and it is outside of you. When you come to know yourselves, then you will become known, and you will realize that it is you who are the sons of the living Father. But if you will not know yourselves, you dwell in poverty and it is you who are that poverty."

Here you have a resume of everything that this book has explained. For Jesus clearly tells you that poverty comes from you, when you don't know yourself. That is, when you repeat the same behaviors, while refusing to correct them, observe them from another person's perspective, and see who you really are, beyond your own self-image.

As Jesus said, once you know yourself, "You will realize that it is you who are the sons of the living Father", meaning, a creator of worlds — a small god within your own world.

It is actually sad that many modern christians interpret the law of attraction as something from the devil, because Jesus was always very explicit in saying that we are the owners of our own outcomes, and we alone create our results.

HOW TO GET LUCKY: HOW TO CHANGE YOUR MIND AND GET ANYTHING IN LIFE

Entering the kingdom of God, quite clearly, means owning that responsibility, as a co-creator. Reason why Jesus said: "The Kingdom is inside of you, and it is outside of you".

Jesus showed you the path and the bridge between the two realities of the kingdom.

You access the kingdom inside of you, by acting 'like little children', when they play with their imagination. And you then access the kingdom outside of you, when you are able to manifest what you previously imagined.

The ancient scriptures always explain in allegories and metaphors, and as many scholars noticed already, it is the modern man that interprets such scriptures quite literally. And that's where the problem is — a misinterpretation and institutional dogma.

The ancient ones always spoke in symbolic ways.

Chapter 46 — The Most Powerful Beliefs.

Our subconscious mind tends to form patterns based on memories. And so, we can shift the focus of those patterns by exercising our imagination with new memories.

Studies show that it takes about 66 days to a whole year, for us to change habits. Therefore, if we can reprogram our self-beliefs with new values and expectations, we will eventually have "a new mind" within those 66 days.

If this new mind is programmed with all the things we wish to have, we can literally get anything in life.

Luck will then seem natural, as we will attract the people, the knowledge, the opportunities, and even the traumas and disappointments — any and all resources that we need in order to reach what in our mind was made possible already.

Once we accomplish those things, it will feel like a *déjà vu*.

The more we reprogram ourselves with new thoughts and new habits, the less power our old program will have over us. Because a habit is just a coalesced set of thoughts, emotions and behaviors that have been automated to conserve energy.

The easier it is to do the new things we want to do, and imagine ourselves having the things we wish to have, and all the luck that requires, the stronger our new habits will be. As a result, our personal magnetism towards those things, will also be clearer and stronger.

The only difference between the kings and the peasants of the past, is that the kings had a strong vision of their goals. History books show us exactly that. They knew what they wanted, and they envisioned themselves having it, far before they had anything. Then, as history also shows, they attracted the right opportunities, allies, and influence.

All great leaders, from Alexander the Great, to Atila and Hannibal, had this characteristic in them, and which, quite often, manifested in their speech and their confidence.

You must believe that you can own an empire before you can conquer it.

Looking back in time, it does seem that they attracted many favorable opportunities. That is, at least, how historians describe such leaders. As if they were all lucky. But we need only to have a look on the things they said, to understand how they created such luck.

Hannibal (born in today's Tunisia) said:

- "I will either find a way or create one";

- "Words are living things. They have personality, perspective, and purpose";

- "The moment to which you do not look forward, will come as a surprise."

Alexander the Great (born in today's Macedonia), said the following:

- "Through every generation of the human race there has been a constant war, a war with fear. Those who have the courage to conquer it are made free and those who are conquered by it are made to suffer until they have the courage to defeat it, or death takes them";

- "There is nothing impossible to the one who will try";

- "With the right attitude, self imposed limitations will vanish".

Last but not least, Atila (born in today's Hungary) said this:

- "It takes less courage to criticize the decisions of others than to stand by your own";

HOW TO GET LUCKY: HOW TO CHANGE YOUR MIND AND GET ANYTHING IN LIFE

- "Superficial goals lead to superficial results".

Now, taking into consideration what these great leaders said, I want you to create your own empire. This would be a collection of all the things you wish to have in your life — marriage, car, trips, house, wealth, etc.

You will do this by creating a laptop wallpaper with a collection of images, that you will then put in your computer, to look at it every time you open it and every time you close it.

You must keep yourself disciplined in the pursuit of your goals, because as Jim Rohn Said, "We must all suffer from one of two pains: the pain of discipline or the pain of regret. The difference is discipline weighs ounces while regret weighs tons."

The future is in your hands — you create the 'kingdom' you wish to experience, and all the luck you need will come your way.

Book Review Request

Dear Reader,

Thank you for purchasing this book!

I would love to know your opinion.

Writing a book review helps in understanding readers and also has an impact on other reader's purchasing decisions. Your opinion matters.

Please write a book review! Your kindness is greatly appreciated!

Books Written By The Author

- 66 Days to Change Your Life: 12 Steps to Effortlessly Remove Mental Blocks, Reprogram Your Brain and Become a Money Magnet

- A New Way of Being: How to Rewire Your Brain and Take Control of Your Life

- Codex Illuminatus: Quotes & Sayings of Dan Desmarques

- Collective Consciousness: How to Transcend Mass Consciousness and Become One With the Universe

- Deception: When Everything You Know about God is Wrong

- Find Your Flow: Find Your Flow: How to Get Wisdom and Knowledge from God

- Holistic Psychology: 77 Secrets about the Mind That They Don't Want You to Know

- How to Change the World: The Path of Global Ascension Through Consciousness

- How to Get Lucky: How to Change Your Mind and Get Anything in Life

- Psychology: 77 Secrets about the Mind That They Don't Want You to Know

- Religious Leadership: The 8 Rules Behind Successful Congregations

- Spiritual Warfare: What You Need to Know About Overcoming Adversity

- Technocracy: The New World Order of the Illuminati and The Battle Between Good and Evil

- The 10 Laws of Transmutation: The Multidimensional Power of Your Subconscious Mind

- The 14 Karmic Laws of Love: How to Develop a Healthy and Conscious Relationship With Your Soulmate

- The Antichrist: The Grand Plan of Total Global Enslavement Holistic

- The Evil Within: The Spiritual Battle in Your Mind

- The Hidden Language of God: How to Find a Balance Between Freedom and Responsibility

- The Secret Beliefs of The Illuminati: The Complete Truth About Manifesting Money Using The Law of Attraction That Is Being Hidden From You

- The Secret Empire: The Hidden Truth Behind the Power Elite and the Knights of the New World Order

- The Secret Science of the Soul: How to Transcend Common Sense and Get What You Really Want From Life

- The Spiritual Mechanics of Love: Secrets They Don't Want You to Know about Understanding and Processing Emotions

- Your Full Potential: How to Overcome Fear and Solve Any Problem

- Your Soul Purpose: Reincarnation and the Spectrum of Consciousness in Human Evolution

- Uncommon: Transcending the Lies of the Mental Health Industry

About the Publisher

This book was published by 22Lions.com.
Follow us at Facebook.com/22lions

www.ingramcontent.com/pod-product-compliance
Lightning Source LLC
Chambersburg PA
CBHW070540170426
43200CB00011B/2497